Airigami

REALISTIC ORIGAMI AIRCRAFT

ELMER A. NORVELL

DOVER PUBLICATIONS, INC.
MINEOLA, NEW YORK

For My Angel

Bibliographical Note

This Dover edition, first published in 2009, is a slightly altered republication of *Airigamido,* originally published by Elmer A. Norvell in 2006.

Library of Congress Cataloging-in-Publication Data

Norvell, Elmer A.
    Airigami : realistic origami aircraft / Elmer A. Norvell.
        p. cm.
    Includes bibliographical references.
    ISBN-13: 978-0-486-47502-8 (pbk.)
    ISBN-10: 0-486-47502-6 (pbk.)
    1. Paper airplanes. 2. Origami. I. Title.

TL778.N67 2009
736'.982—dc22

                                                    2009037223

Manufactured in the United States by Courier Corporation
47502601
www.doverpublications.com

Note

The accompanying CD-ROM contains 55 bonus images saved in both 300-dpi, high-resolution, and 72-dpi, Internet-ready formats; folding instructions for three additional aircraft; and 24 "skins," complete with markings, that can be printed out and folded.

Within the "Images" folder on the CD, you will find four additional folders: "JPG," containing the 72-dpi image files; "Hi-Res JPG," containing the 300-dpi image files; "Skins," and "Extras," containing the folding instructions.

If you want to add your name (or a friend's name) to an aircraft, you can use your favorite graphics program. All of the skins are also contained in a .ppt file for use in Microsoft PowerPoint, if you prefer editing in that program.

Printer setups vary from computer to computer, so you may have to adjust landmarks or change printer settings to make the printouts match the fold lines exactly. Be patient and always refer to the diagrams in the book as the primary instructions.

Also included is the Dover Design Manager, an easy-to-use image editing program that will allow you to view, rotate, flip, and print the images.

For technical support, contact:
Telephone: 1 (617) 249-0245
Fax: 1 (617) 249-0245
Email: dover@artimaging.com
Internet: **http://www.dovertechsupport.com**

The fastest way to receive technical support is via email or the Internet.

About the Author

Elmer A. Norvell is a Professional Engineer with over 24 years service in the US Military. He is a private pilot and ultra-light aircraft test pilot. His hobbies include mathematics, scuba diving, and running 100-mile marathons (with a best time of less than 21 hours!).

He lives in Pike Road, Alabama with his wife, also a marathoner and his son, who is an Eagle Scout and a drummer.

Introduction

I love folding paper. Paper animals, paper buildings, paper insects, but most of all I love folding paper airplanes. You see, I am also passionate about airplanes. I have flown aircraft of many shapes and sizes from free-flight, rubber-band powered balsa stick and tissue models, radio-controlled electrics and gas, full-scale private general aviation, and even once, I was at the controls of an actual full-scale military F-16 Fighting Falcon doing an axial roll at 30,000 feet!

Origami is the perfect medium to express my rational, mathematical character and my artistic, child-like imagination. It is still mystical to me how birds take flight and manage to land with pinpoint accuracy on a wire seemingly effortlessly. Even knowing Bernoulli principles and myriads of mathematical and engineering reasons for making flight possible, I still think there is something magical about flight. I find the same magic in folding paper. Even though rationally I can see the logic of the folds, it still surprises me when a two-dimensional sheet of nothing converts into a three-dimensional object in my hands.

Folding is also a fun way to pass the time and the number of models you can make is only limited by how much paper you have available. Paper never seems to be a problem with all the junk mail and advertisements out there. I have had great fun folding models in waiting rooms and have gotten into some good-humored trouble with mothers whose children toss the airplanes around in delight.

I hope you share my enthusiasm for creating and flying great looking, realistic paper aircraft.

"T.J."
Elmer A. Norvell

Additional information:

The designs in this compilation are my own. However, I have generously borrowed and adapted techniques found in numerous other origami works listed in the bibliography. All drafting of the diagrams is also by my hand. I have made every attempt to make the drawings accurate and easy to follow. The majority of these designs are Intermediate to Complex. Only through dedication and repetition can one expect to get quality results. Because the paper used in these designs is available and on many occasions free, creating excellent flying and static models is only limited to the time one spends in practice. For clarification of any designs or errors in the diagrams, please send comments to **tjsairigamido@aol.com**

Special thanks to John Montroll, for his advice, and Mark Kennedy for his enthusiasm. My most heartfelt appreciation to my wife, Jeanell Norvell, PhD, for her excellent photography for this book and her enduring encouragement.

My Origami philosophy:
1. Maximum efficiency with minimum effort. (Elegance) Achieve a rational design through natural folding rhythm to achieve a realistic and functional model.
2. Mutual welfare and benefit. Create an environment of mutual respect among designers and folders that synergistically promotes and elevates the art of origami and the "Peace of Paper."

Contents

Symbols/Structures

Lift

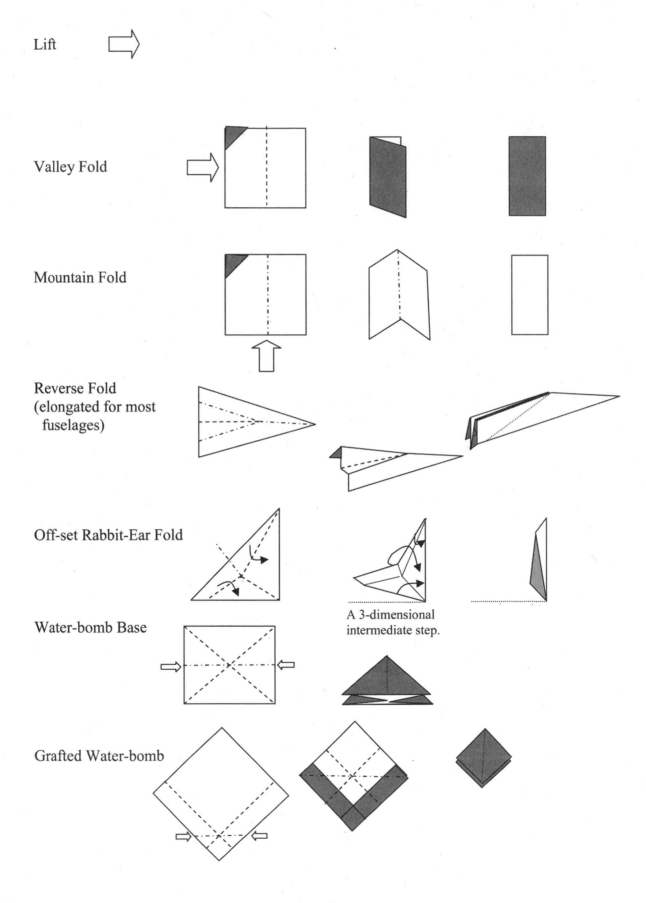

Valley Fold

Mountain Fold

Reverse Fold
(elongated for most
fuselages)

Off-set Rabbit-Ear Fold

A 3-dimensional
intermediate step.

Water-bomb Base

Grafted Water-bomb

Flight Principles

Flight Worthiness of Paper Models - Gravity, Thrust, Lift, and Drag

Gravity and Thrust

Gravity and Thrust are mostly fixed. To change gravity significantly you must get out of Earth's gravity by going out in space or living on a different planet. Currently there are not many options. Thrust is limited by the strength and technique of whoever is flying the model. There is some difference in experienced paper airplane pilots, however mostly this is a matter of practice and trial and error. Launching aircraft at the correct attitude and when outside launching into the wind may improve the flight duration and performance.

Lift

Most efficient lifting bodies tend to be slow and have a lot of inherent drag. The lifting foil is a good example of a duration-type paper plane.

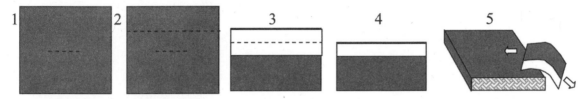

Flying Foil – start with any square on Step 5 bend around the sharp corner of a desk to make dihedral curve (for stability).

6 Gently push and foil will fly.

The foil is effective because it maximizes wing area by eliminating the fuselage and other control surfaces and projections. There are not many scale examples of these. Good sources of these type full-scale aircraft are the X-Planes programs. The X-20 Dyna-Soar and the X-23 Prime, X-24 (A,B and C), X-30 A, X-33, X-38 and the X-45A UCAV are all good examples of lifting body designs. These aircraft are much more difficult to trim and control than dart-type conventional jets. They are not as aesthetically appealing nor as well known as conventional aircraft. The lifting body design is important and has led to the development of the reusable space shuttle.

Dart-type jets do not rely on lift as much as they do thrust. Designs include F-16, F16-XL, XB-70 Valkyrie, X-29, and SAAB Gripen which are likely the best flyers in this book. They are fast and can fly long distances. They have relatively low drag and slightly less wing area. They are a good combination of speed and duration.

Drag

Drag is undesirable and inhibits flight speed and duration for paper airplanes. More projections such as the XB-70 Valkyrie (page 35) compared to the F-16XL (page 25) equates to more drag on the XB-70. However, larger wing area to weight ratios cause increased drag and reduces overall speed.

(see **How to Trim/Airplane Terms** *page 111* for additional information)

Concorde

The Concorde was the first and only commercial jet to cruise at speeds faster than the speed of sound. This Mach 2 plus aircraft was the product of cooperation between the Sud-Aviation of France and the British Aircraft Corporation (BAC). This SST (Super-Sonic Transport) began operation in 1976 and flew up to 144 passengers each flight until it was taken out of service 25 years later.

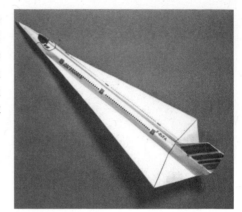

Start with 5''x 5" (square) colored/printed side down

1. Fold in half on diagonal. Unfold.

2. Fold raw edges to center on both sides.

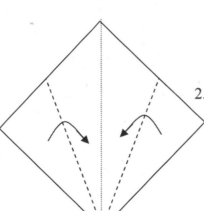

3. This creates a kite base. (Guess why it is called a kite-base.) Fold in half. Leave folded.

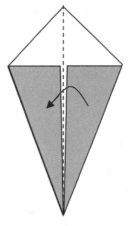

4. Valley fold Front and Back.

5. Valley fold wing. Repeat on reverse side. Turn to the right.

10

6. Reverse fold rudder by pulling it
   through the fuselage. The pivot point is at the apex of the hidden paper (point A).

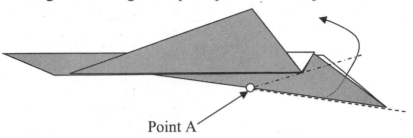

Point A

7. Reverse fold rudder in half.

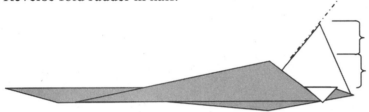

8. Pull wings down to right angles (90 degrees) to fuselage. Shape nose. Fold down on elevators slightly to trim for flight.

9. 3-Dimensional Detail

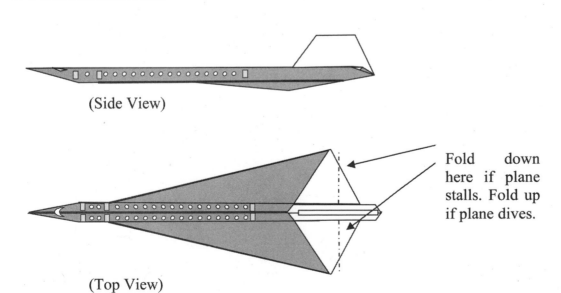

(Side View)

(Top View)

Fold down here if plane stalls. Fold up if plane dives.

11

Boeing X-45A UCAV

The Boeing X-45A Unmanned Combat Aerial Vehicle (UCAV) is the test bed for combat aircraft flown without a pilot on-board. The vehicle can be directed via satellite control or fly autonomously (self-guided) by pre-programmed computer. The vehicle is stealthy and there is no political pressure to rescue a pilot if things go wrong. Could the future be combat airplanes without pilots in them?

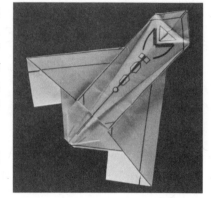

1. Start with square paper colored side down. Fold and unfold along long diagonal.

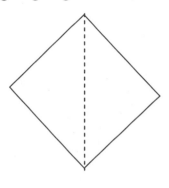

2. Fold and unfold to mark locations.

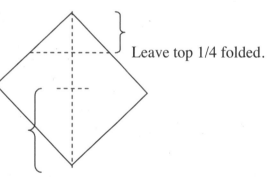

Leave top 1/4 folded.

3. Valley fold and unfold fuselage

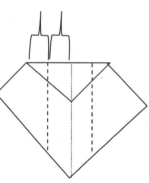

4. Valley-fold and unfold the wings.

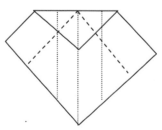

5. Fold up the tail section then fold back the exhaust.

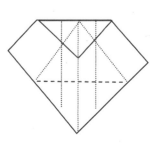

6. Fold back exhaust.

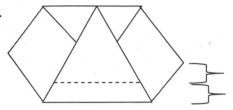

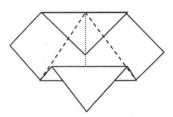

7. Refold wings

8. Narrow wings by valley folding trailing edge.

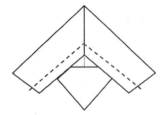

9. Valley-fold tail.

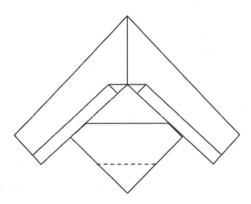

10. Valley-fold first then mountain-fold (fold back out) the fuselage. Note the pre-folds indicate where you should fold.

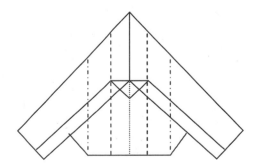

11. Valley-fold and tuck gray shaded area in tail.

12. Fold fuselage in half and turn model as shown.

13. Fold up fuselage.

14. Reverse fold nose

15. Fold out and shape. Nose should be valley-folded as shown.

Top View

Front View (now you know why radar has trouble seeing it!)

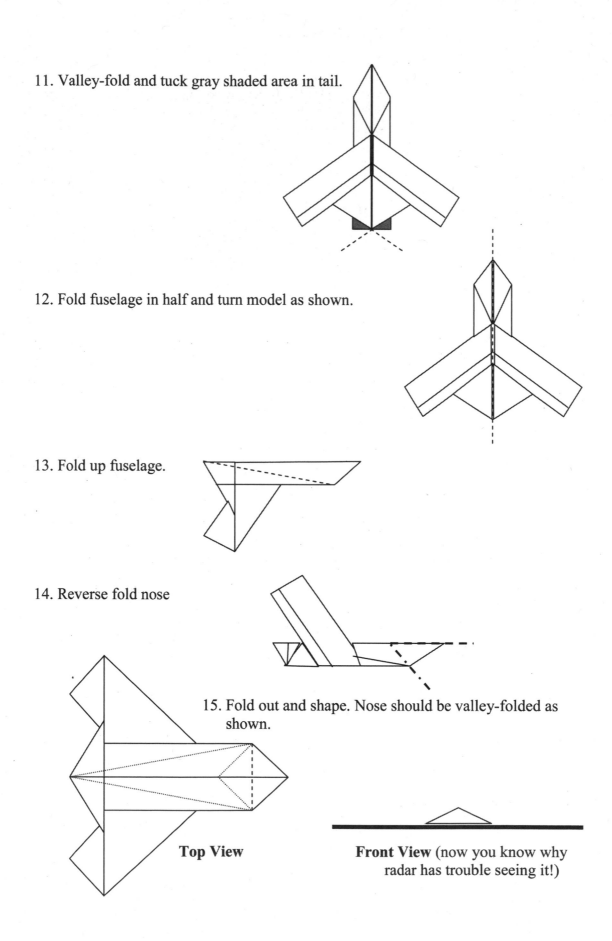

AURORA

This top-secret aircraft may or may not exist. No verified sightings have been made of this "Black Project." The depiction here is my fantasy of Bill Sweetman's interpretation of what this pulse-jet may look like, but feel free to come up with your own variation. The "truth" is out there…

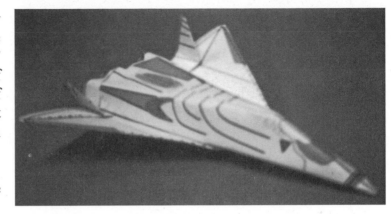

Start with square colored/printed side down.

1.

Fold and unfold.

2.

Mark center by creasing.

3.

Fold top edge to crease.

4.

Fold diagonal bisector.

5.

6.

7.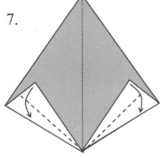

8.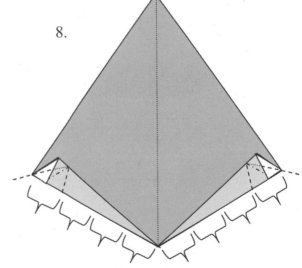

Off-set Rabbit Ear folds.

9.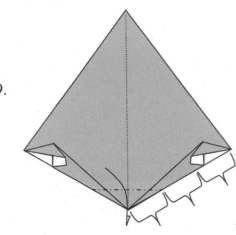

Mountain-fold, turn over.

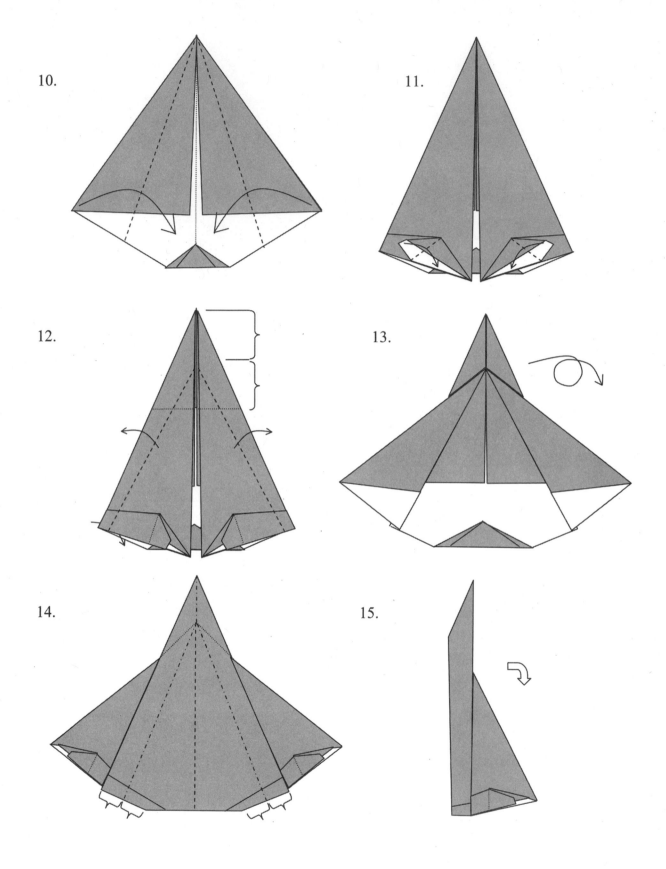

10.

11.

12.

13.

14.

15.

16.

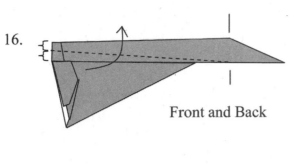

Front and Back

17.

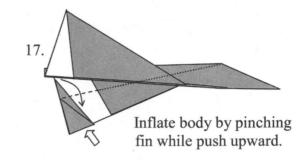

Inflate body by pinching fin while push upward.

18.

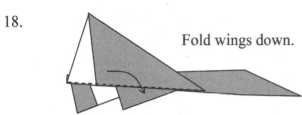

Fold wings down.

19.

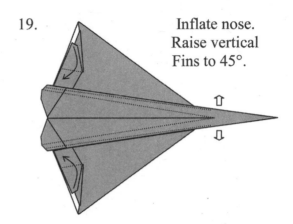

Inflate nose. Raise vertical Fins to 45°.

20. Match to 3-D Drawings

Side View

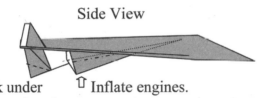

Tuck under dark gray triangle to lock fuselage. ⇧ Inflate engines.

Top View

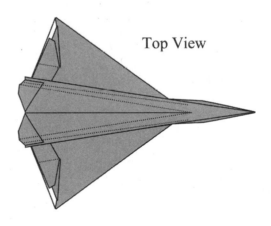

Front View

Rear View

F-16 Fighting Falcon

The F-16 Fighting Falcon developed by General Dynamics is one of the most prolific fighter aircraft flying today. Over 90 countries have this airplane in their inventory, over 4,000 have been produced. The F-16 flies at over Mach-2 (twice the speed of sound).

Start with 8.5" x 11" rectangle colored side down.

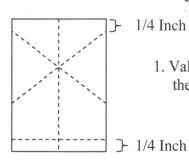

}─ 1/4 Inch

}─ 1/4 Inch

1. Valley fold along dashed lines, then unfold. (4 folds total).

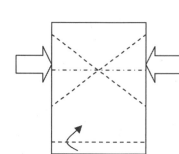

2. Mountain Fold along dash-dot line, then unfold and push sides to produce the following diagram. Push up on pre-fold at the bottom and leave folded.

3. Lift one layer and fold to the left.

Expanded View

4. Valley fold two diagonals.

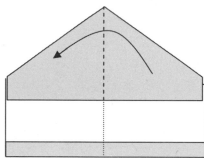

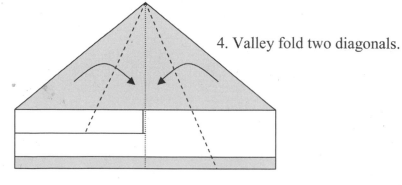

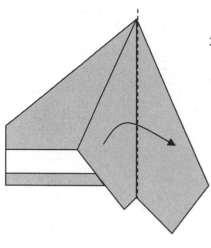

5. Lift layer and return it to the right side.

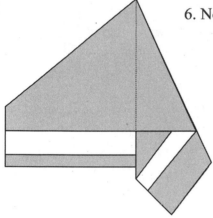

6. Now repeat steps 3, 4, and 5 on the left side.

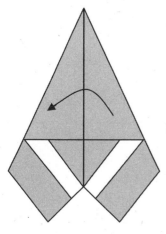

7. The result should look like this. Next, lift the top right layer and fold over to the left.

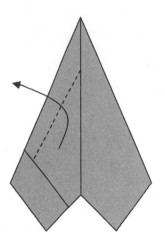

8. Valley fold the wing along the dashed line. (Just the top layer)

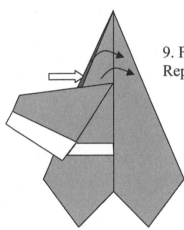

9. Fold the top two layers over to the right side. Repeat Step 8 on the right side.

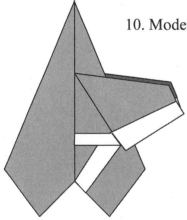

10. Model should look like this. Go to the next step.

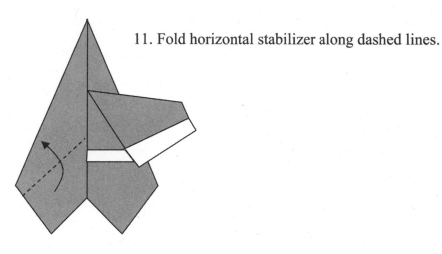

11. Fold horizontal stabilizer along dashed lines.

12. Valley fold on both dashed lines. Do Line 1 first then do Line 2. (Note the fold on Line 1 is small, just peel it down as far as it will go. Take your time to avoid tearing.)

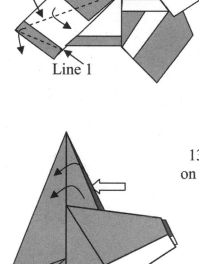

Line 2

Line 1

13. Lift two layers and fold to the left and repeat steps 11 and 12 on the right side.

14. Lift top layer and fold to the right.

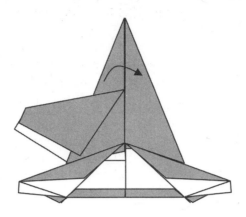

15. Turn the model over. (Colored side up.)

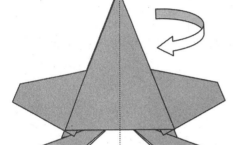

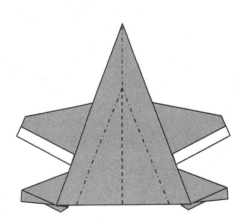

16. Perform a reverse fold along the dashed lines. This is the hardest part of this design. It is easier to do the mountain folds along the colored part of the right side of the fuselage first, then squeeze the left side to complete the fold. (See the practice folds at the front of the book.)

17. Give the model a quarter turn to the right to make it look like the diagram. Valley fold along the dashed line through two layers. Repeat on the backside.

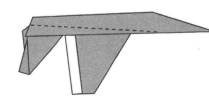

22

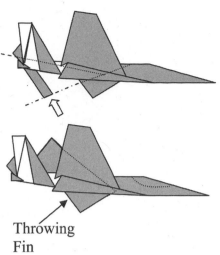

18. Pull up on the left most section under the belly of the aircraft (shaded area) until the vertical stabilizer appears as shown in the next diagram. This is the easiest way to perform this reverse fold.

19. Note new location of vertical stabilizer. Hold on to the throwing fin and pull down on the wing until it is level with the base of the fuselage. Repeat in the rear.

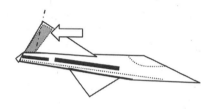

Throwing
Fin

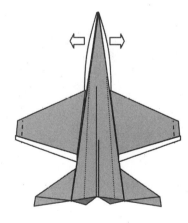

20. Reach gently under the vertical stabilizer and pull out the trapped paper as far as it will go in order to make the rudder. Note: colors are reversed to show location of trapped paper. (Squeeze together after pulling out.)

21. Turn model so that the cockpit faces you and shape the nose. Valley fold the tiny triangles on the tail and tuck inside the top layer of paper.

Valley fold wing tips to make missile rails.

Holding the throwing fin, give the model a mild toss.

3-Dimensional shaping instructions.

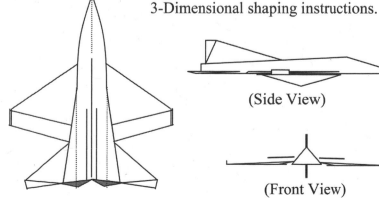

(Side View)

(Front View)

Optional scale-like wing design. Model flies in either configuration.

Mountain-fold along lateral line and valley-fold small distance as shown through all layers. (This actually looks and works better than the more complicated double reverse folds along the same lines on wings, see Raptor instruction steps 10-12 (on page 57), if you would like to give it a try.)

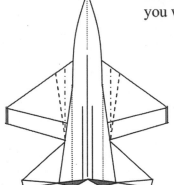 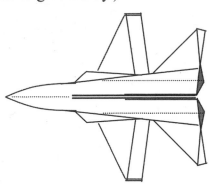

F-16XL Experimental

The F-16XL Experimental is a one of kind F-16 fitted with a delta wing. This aircraft was flown by a female test pilot, Marta R. Bohn-Meyer. Though never put into production, the aircraft demonstrates the versatility of the basic F-16 design.

Start with 8.5" x 11" rectangle colored side down

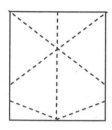

1. Valley fold along dashed lines, then unfold. (5 folds total)

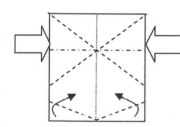

2. Mountain Fold along dash-dot line, then unfold and push sides to produce the following diagram. Push up on pre-folds at the bottom and leave folded.

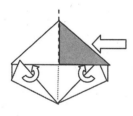

3. This produces a modified water-bomb base. Tuck both bottom flaps under all layers. Lift top layer and fold to the left.

Expanded View

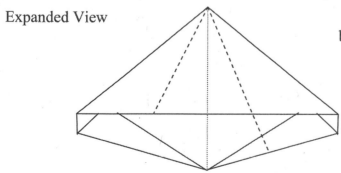

4. Valley fold two diagonal bisectors.

25

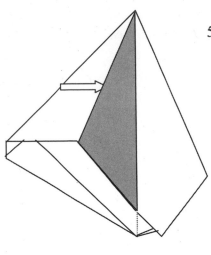

5. Lift layer and return it to the right side.

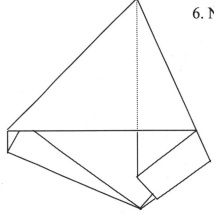

6. Now repeat steps 3, 4, and 5 on the left side.

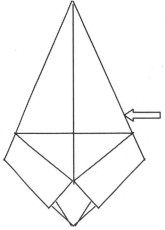

7. The result should look like this. Next, lift the top right layer and fold over to the left.

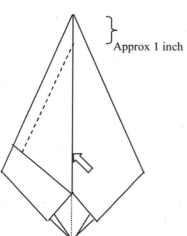

8. Valley fold the wing along the dashed line. (Just the top layer)

Approx 1 inch

9. Fold the top layer over to the right side.

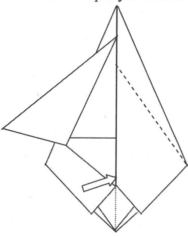

10. Model should look like this.
Valley fold the top layer back to the right.

11. Mountain fold and tuck the top layer under the bottom paper as shown.

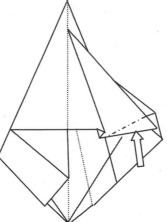

12. Repeat steps 7 through 11 on the left side.

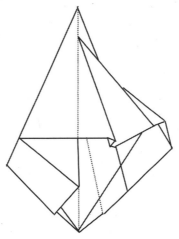

13. Model should look like this. Turn the model over.

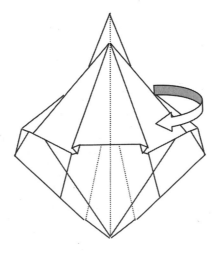

14. Reverse fold through all layers and allow the model to collapse sideways.

Perform another reverse fold inside the last one to make a boxy fuselage. (optional)

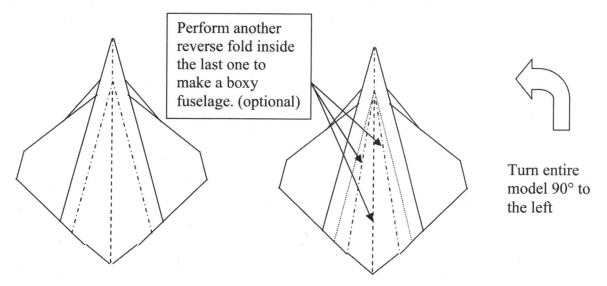

Turn entire model 90° to the left

15. Reverse fold rudder by pulling up on paper shown at arrow.

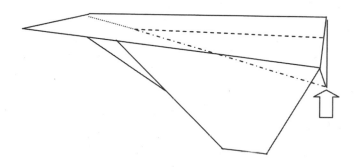

16. Push fold on the facing side along the mountain fold lines. Repeat on back side.

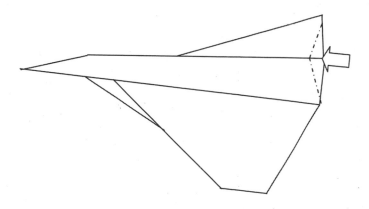

17. Valley fold wings along lateral lines. Bend up through all layers and then back down to 90 degrees (Perpendicular). Repeat on back side.

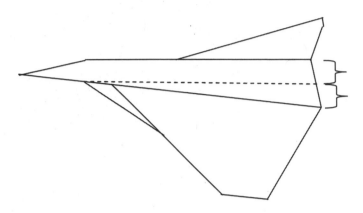

18. Reverse fold rudder tip.

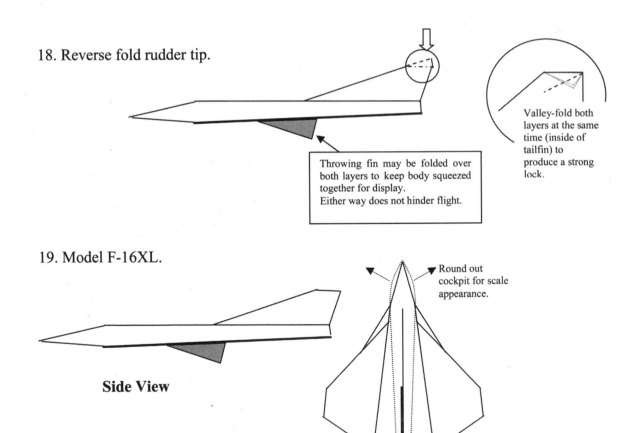

Throwing fin may be folded over both layers to keep body squeezed together for display.
Either way does not hinder flight.

Valley-fold both layers at the same time (inside of tailfin) to produce a strong lock.

19. Model F-16XL.

Round out cockpit for scale appearance.

Side View

Top View

SAAB Gripen/Rafale

Designed for my college friend Rick, a Viggen and Gripen pilot. Sweden prides itself on producing their own aircraft. As a result of WWII, Swedish aircraft are designed for short take offs and landings which enable them to be launched from unconventional surfaces such as remote roadways and unimproved surfaces. Eliminating the requirement for airports, the Swedes can disperse their aircraft throughout the country.

Start with 8.5" x 11" rectangle colored side down

1. Fold along lines, then unfold, except for the two bottom valley folds.

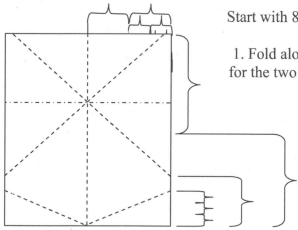

2. Mountain Fold along dash-dot line, then unfold and push sides to produce the following diagram. Mountain fold as shown at the bottom two diagonals and leave folded.

3. Lift top layer and fold over to the left.

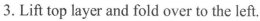

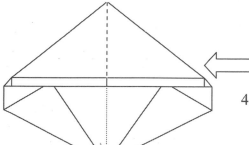

4. Valley fold both bisectors.

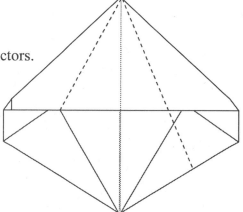

5. Valley fold wing.

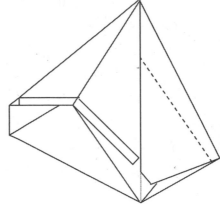

6. Offset-rabbit ear fold the canard winglet.

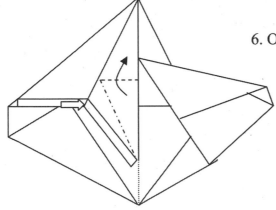

7. Fold along same angle as the wing.

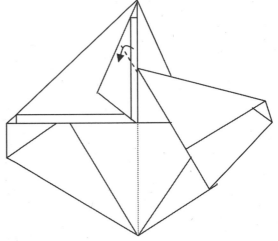

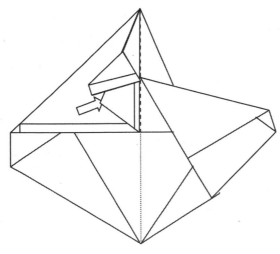

8. Fold over top layer.

9. Repeat steps 3 through 8 on the left side.

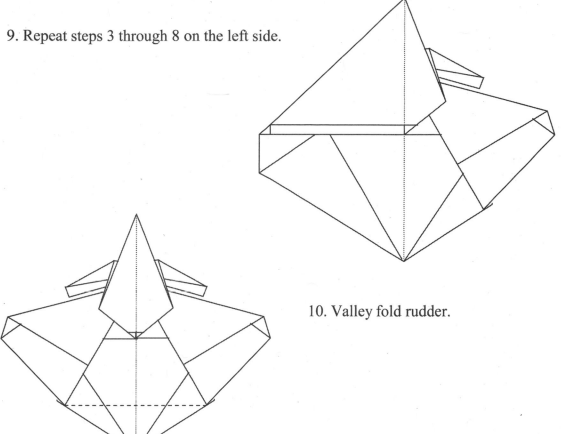

10. Valley fold rudder.

11. Double Reverse fold all layers as indicated. It helps to pre-fold along the dotted lines. Model should collapse. Ensure both side are symmetrical.

Turn model 90° to the right.

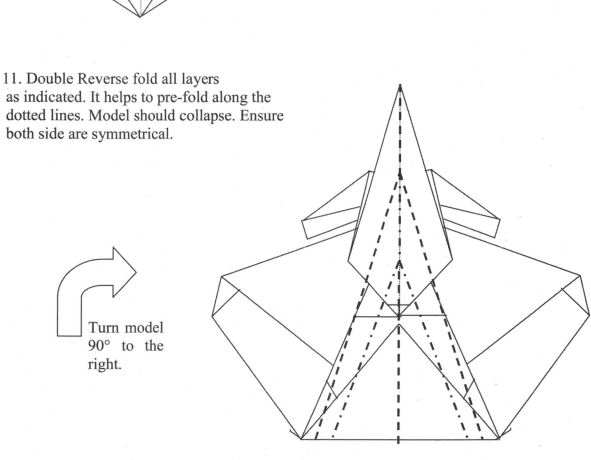

12. Reach under the fuselage and pull out the triangle of paper (shown in gray). You may have to open up the model quite a bit. Squash fold the rudder along the dotted (hidden) line.

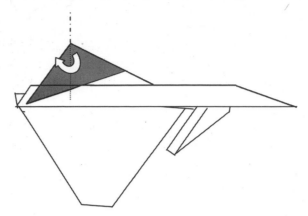

13. Valley fold to 90 degrees. Mountain fold the winglets. Repeat on backside.

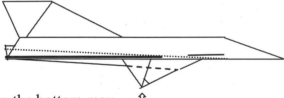

14. Make adjustments to conform to these drawings.

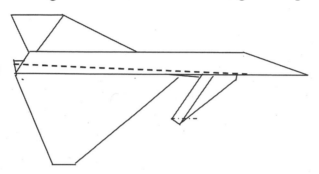

The fin on the bottom may
be left for throwing or bent through all layers
and tucked under the fuselage to make a neater look.

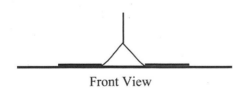

Front View

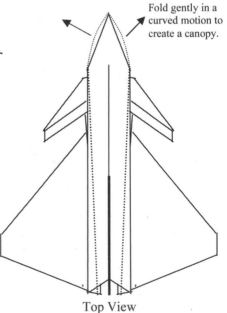

Fold gently in a curved motion to create a canopy.

Top View

XB-70 Valkyrie

Only two XB-70 Valkyries were built. This Mach-3 Bomber was to be a part of the US strategic nuclear delivery system against the former Soviet Union. Sadly, after the destruction of one of the Valkyries during a photo shoot (a chase aircraft was sucked into the XB-70's enormous vertex) the program was cancelled in favor of ICBM missiles. The program became the foundation for the B-1 Lancer. The remaining XB-70 is on display at Wright-Patterson Air Force Base, Ohio. This model is dedicated to Valkyrie pilot, Fitzhugh L. Fulton, Jr.

Start with 8.5" x 11" rectangle colored side down

1. Valley fold. Unfold.
   (3 folds total)

2. Mountain Fold along dash-dot line, then unfold and push sides (Water-Bomb Base). Mountain fold as shown at the bottom two diagonals and leave folded.

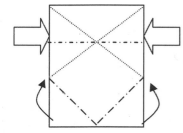

3. Lift top layer and fold to the left.

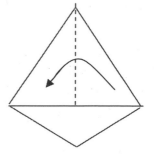

Expanded View

4. Valley fold two diagonal bisectors.

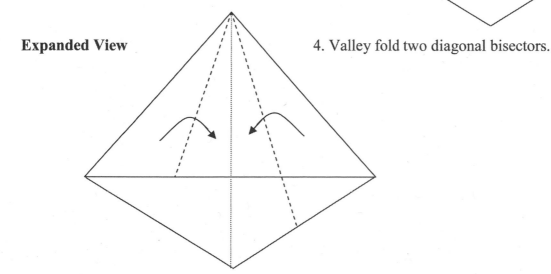

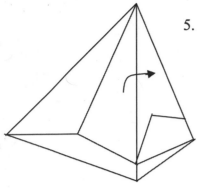

5. Lift layer and return it to the right side.

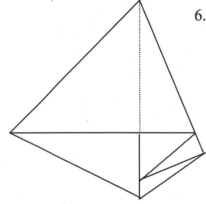

6. Now repeat steps 3, 4, and 5 on the left side.

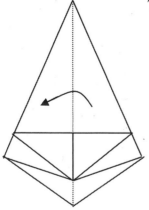

7. The result should look like this. Next, lift the top right layer and fold over to the left.

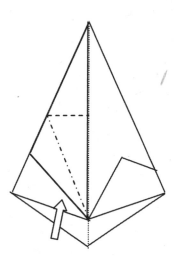

8. Rabbit-ear fold the winglet along the dashed line. (Just the top layer)

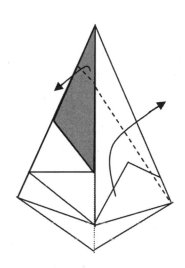

9. Fold the top layer on the right side over to the right. This creates the wing. Fold the winglet on the left down.

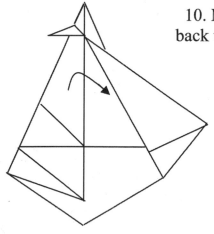

10. Model should look like this. Fold Top layer back to the right and go to the next step.

11. Repeat steps 7 – 10 on the left side.

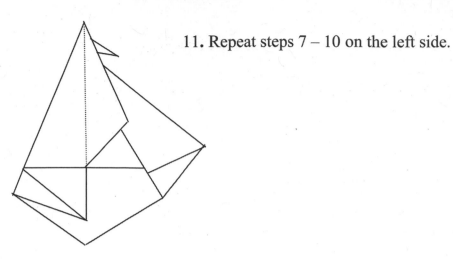

12. Valley-fold along the pre-fold line.

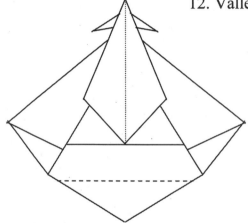

13. Turn the model over.

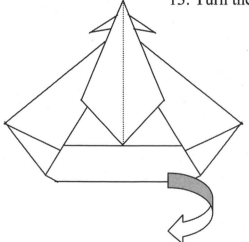

14. Pull out paper and valley-fold diagonals.

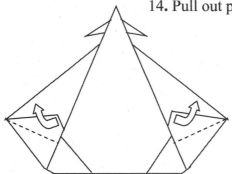

15. Off-set rabbit-ear fold the rudders. Both sides.

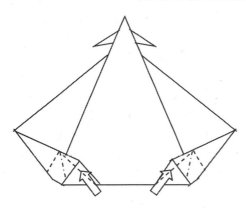

16. Perform reverse fold on the center of the model. This is difficult because there are many layers. Rotate the model to the right.

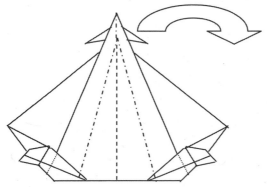

17. Fold up to 90 degrees along valley fold line. Repeat on back.

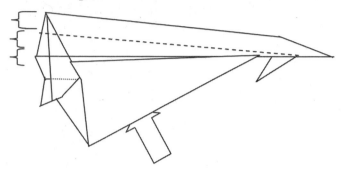

18. Finish model by shaping the nose and bending rudders to perpendicular. Ensure the wings and winglets are in alignment and give the XB-70 Valkyrie a toss.

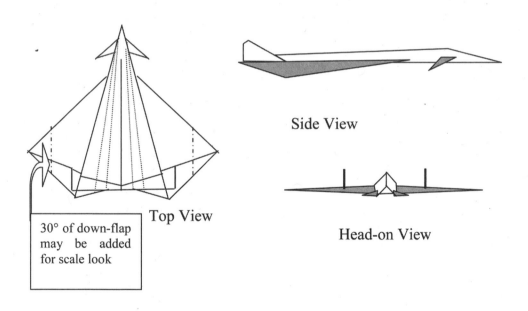

Top View

30° of down-flap may be added for scale look

Side View

Head-on View

Rocket Racer

The Rocket Racer idea is the mind spring of the sponsors of the X-Prize which the StarShipOne designed by Burt Rutan was able to win by creating a spacecraft that could enter low earth atmosphere and return to accomplish the same feat again in two weeks. The Rocket Racers are to be a sort of "NASCAR" race, only using rocket powered aircraft instead of cars.

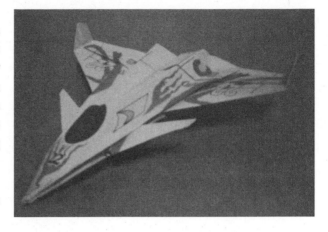

Start with 8.5" x 11" rectangle colored side down

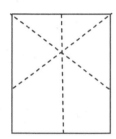

1. Valley fold along dashed lines, then unfold. (3 folds total)

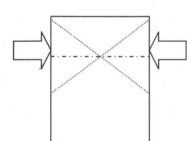

2. Mountain Fold along dash-dot line, then unfold and push sides to produce the following diagram.

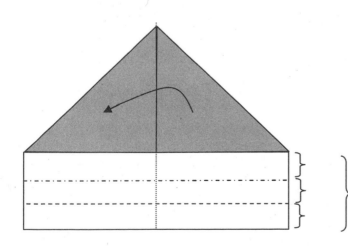

3. Valley fold and mountain fold the bottom. Fold right top flap over to the left side.

4. Valley fold the diagonal bisector.

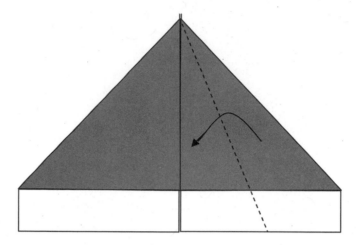

5. Valley fold wing.

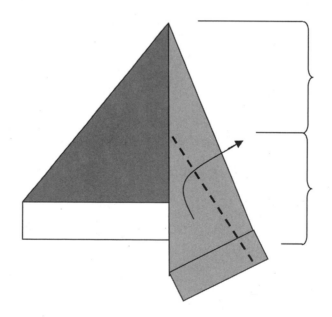

6. Twist fold around point A.

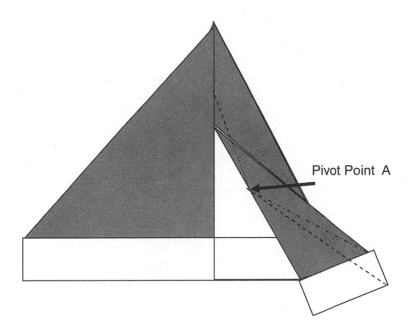

Pivot Point A

7. Stretch fold by pulling down on Point A, located on the bottom layer in the right corner.

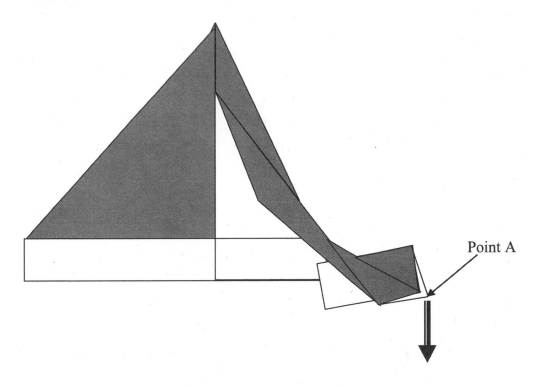

Point A

8. The result should look like this. Create small folds on excess trailing edge paper and tuck into pocket.

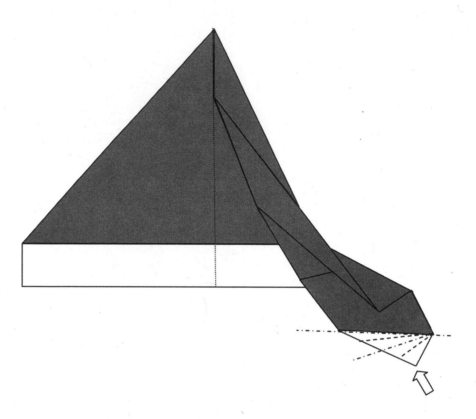

9. Off-set rabbit-ear fold the winglets along the dashed line on left and right side. (Just the top layer)

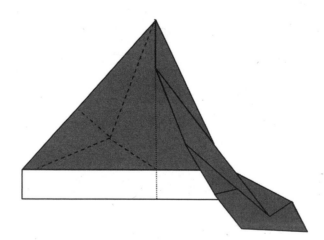

10. Valley fold winglet tip (top layer only), the valley fold winglet.

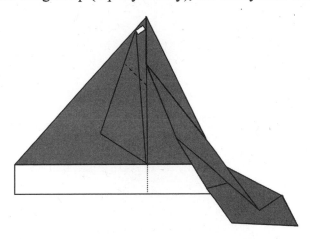

11. Fold over top layer. Repeat steps 3-11 on left side.

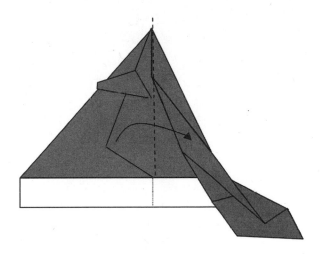

12. Result should look like this. Turn model over.

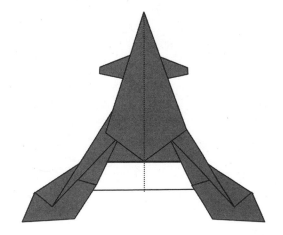

13. Reverse fold through all layers.

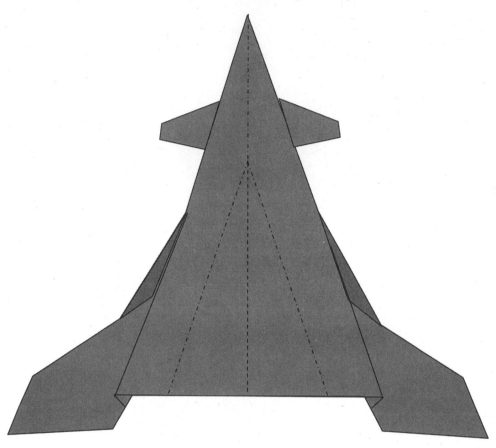

14. Turn sideways and valley fold wings and side of fuselage to 90 degrees. Repeat behind.

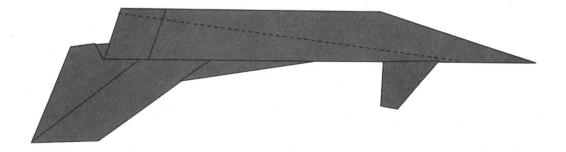

15. Hold middle and push up slightly. Refold along new lines creating a boxy shape to the fuselage.

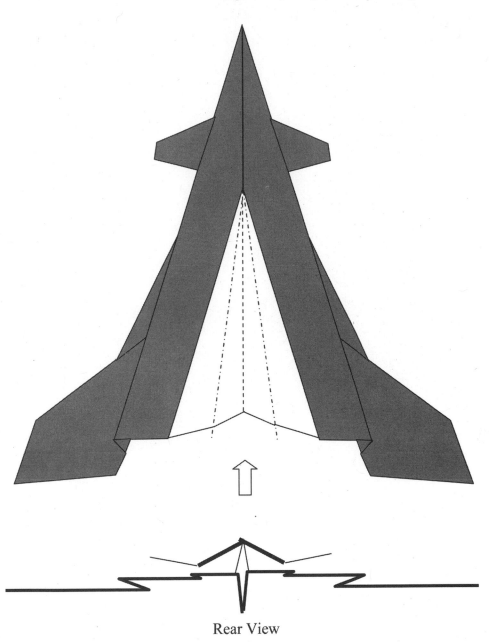

Rear View

16. Fold tip rudders up to 90 degrees. Shape nose and trim to fly.

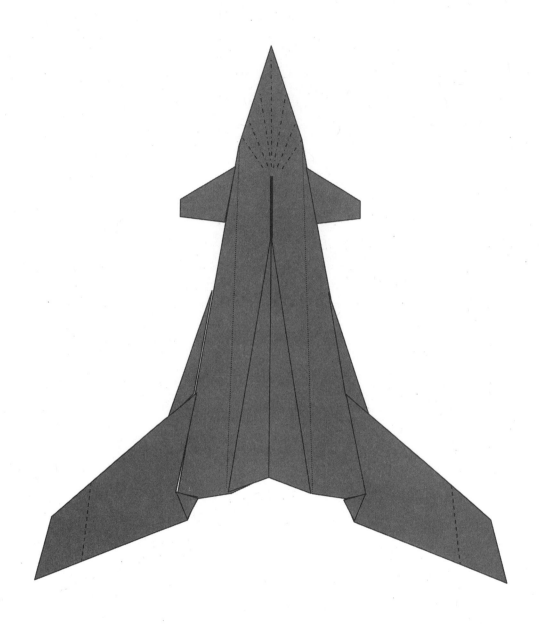

17. Give hard toss.

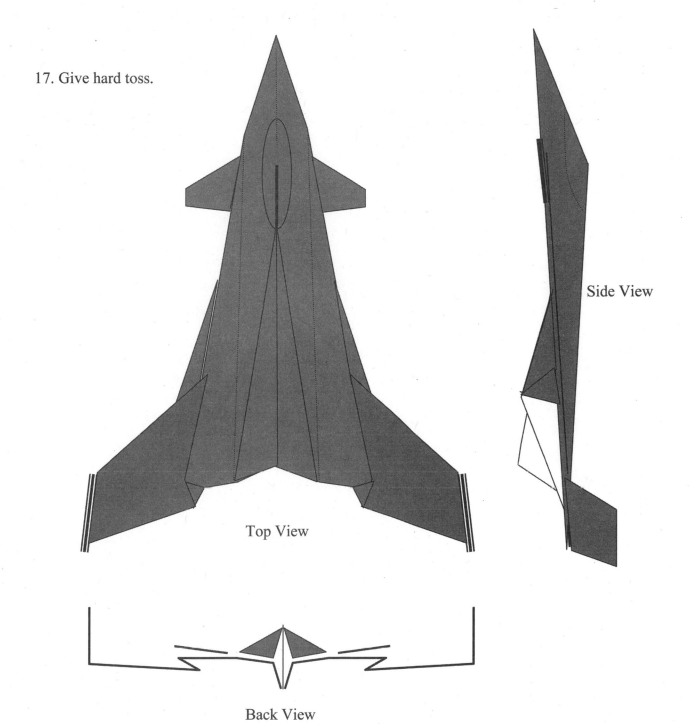

Top View

Side View

Back View

Grumman X-29 Experimental

The Grumman X-29 experimented with forward swept wings to destabilize the aircraft. This instability had the potential to make the aircraft more maneuverable than conventional designs. The actual airplane required over 20 sophisticated computers to keep the plane in control. Fortunately, your paper model only requires a little patience to trim.

Start with 8.5" x 11" rectangle colored side down

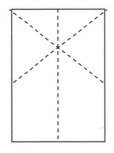

1. Valley fold along dashed lines, then unfold. (3 folds total) I leave 2 or three millimeters of paper on the leading edge. I do not fold quite to the corner diagonals. Experiment if you like or just fold diagonals to the corners as normal. The only thing this affects is the amount of plane on the forward canards.

2. Mountain Fold along dash-dot line, then unfold and push sides to produce the following diagram. Push up on pre-fold at the bottom and leave folded.

3. Lift one layer and fold to the left.

Expanded View

Top Layer Only

4. Valley fold left diagonal to the center. Valley fold right diagonal to the center while pushing up on the bottom flap.

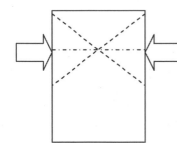

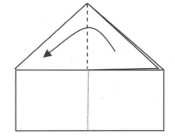

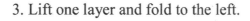

5. Valley fold the piece shown and leave folded.

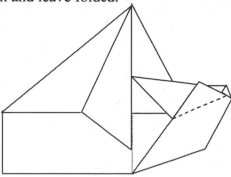

6. Simultaneously fold out from the center and mountain fold the leading edge of the wing. This is a twisting fold used to make the wing gussets. (Pivot Fold)

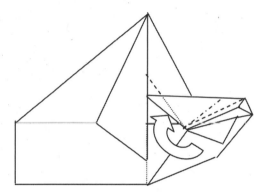

7. Lift layer and return it to the right side.

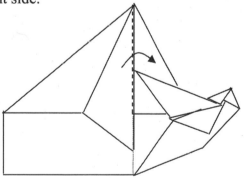

8. Repeat steps 3, 4, and 5 on the left side.

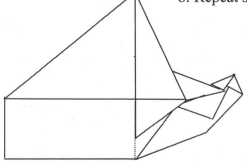

9. The result should look like this. Next, lift the top right layer and fold over to the left.

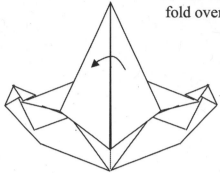

10. Off-set rabbit-ear fold the winglet along the dashed line. (Just the top layer)

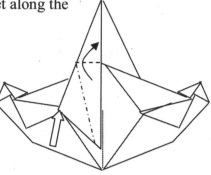

11. Fold the top layer on the right side over to the right. Fold the winglet to the left and as far down as possible.

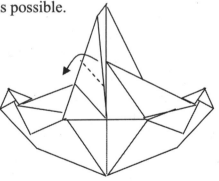

12. Model should look like this. Fold top layer back to the right and go to the next step.

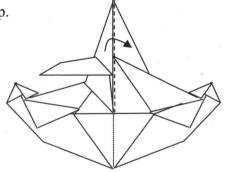

13. Repeat steps 9 – 12 on the left side.

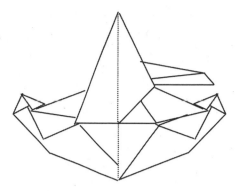

14. The model should look like the figure below. Turn the paper over.

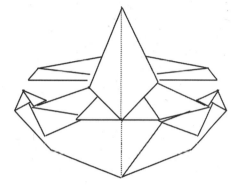

15. Reverse fold as indicated.
Rotate nose to the left.

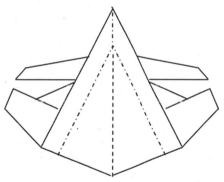

16. Reverse fold the vertical fin by pulling tip up through the fuselage.

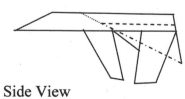

Side View

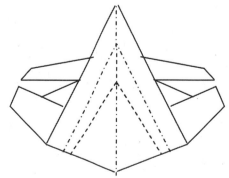

Top View

17. Valley fold where indicated. Then fold out to 90 degrees (horizontal).

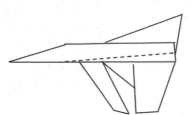 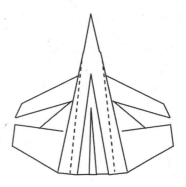

18. Fold canards as indicated and tuck under top layer.

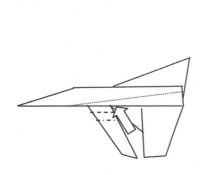 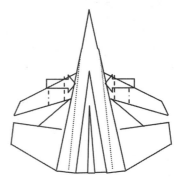

19. Shape nose and intake ducts as indicated.

Ducts can be rounded out with a pen.

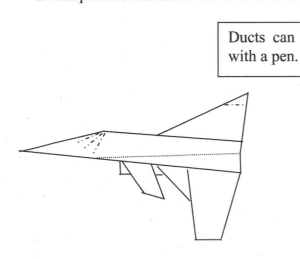 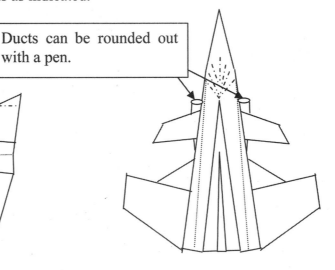

20. Despite its unusual appearance, this model has the potential to fly remarkably well.

F-22 Raptor

The F-22 Raptor can fly supersonic without afterburners and uses stealth technology to achieve air superiority. It is especially adapted for Suppression of Enemy Air Defenses (SEAD) and air-to-air combat. It is the newest addition to the US Air Force, taking the place of the aging F-15 Strike Eagle.

1. Start with 8.5" x 11" rectangle colored or printed (or foil – recommended) side down. Valley fold along dashed lines, then unfold. (6 folds total)

2. Mountain Fold along dash-dot line, then unfold and push sides to produce the following diagram. Push up on pre-fold at the bottom and leave folded.

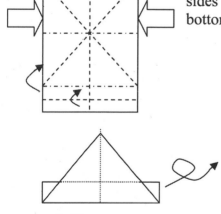

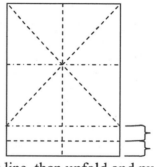

3. Turn over.

4. Reverse fold outside corners.

Expanded View

5. Valley fold diagonal bisecting angles. Top layer only.

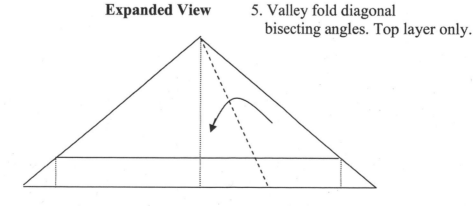

6. Lift layer and move it to the left side.

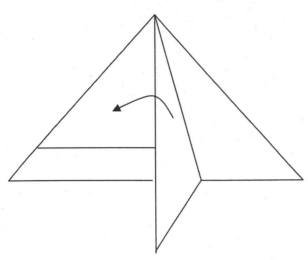

7. Valley fold remaining layer as shown.

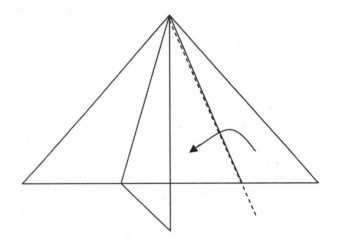

8. Fold left layer back to the right.

9. Repeat steps 5, 6, and 7 on the left side.

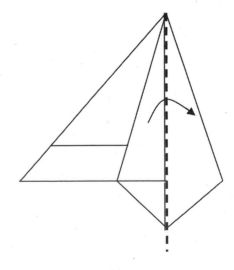

10. The result should look like this. Lift the top right layer and fold over to the left. Thay Yang developed a base similar to this for his F-14 Tomcat in <u>Exotic Paper Airplanes</u>.

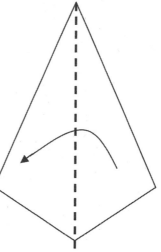

11. Valley fold the wing along the dashed line. (Just the top layer)

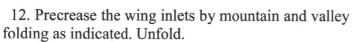

12. Precrease the wing inlets by mountain and valley folding as indicated. Unfold.

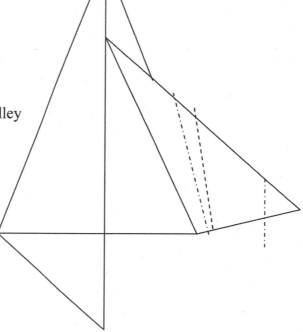

13. Model should look like this. Unfold this section to the right.

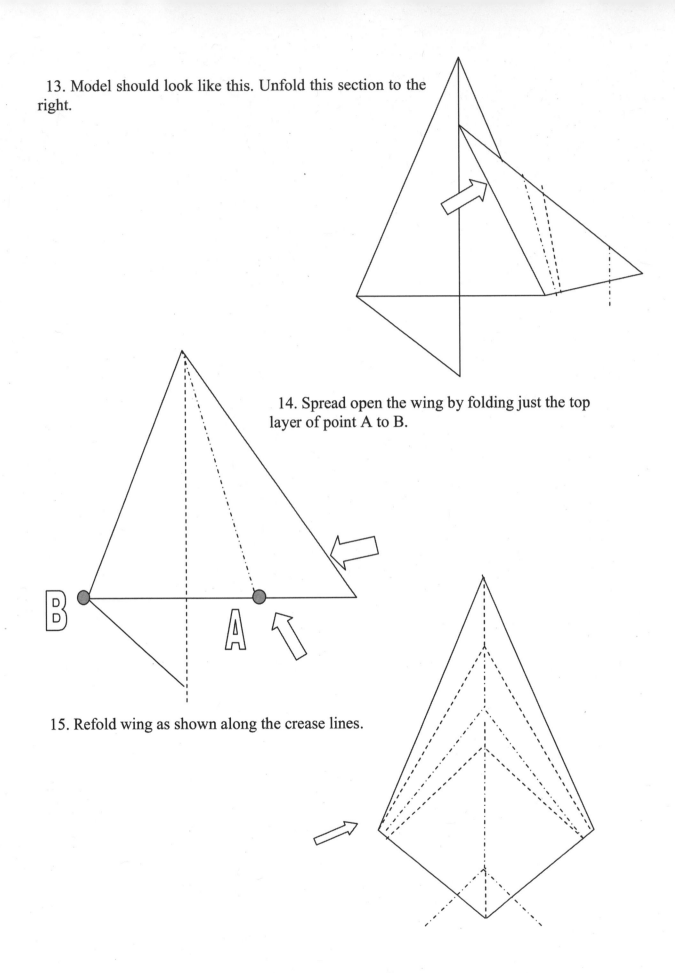

14. Spread open the wing by folding just the top layer of point A to B.

15. Refold wing as shown along the crease lines.

16. Result should look like the diagram. Mountain fold top layer of the trailing edge and tuck.

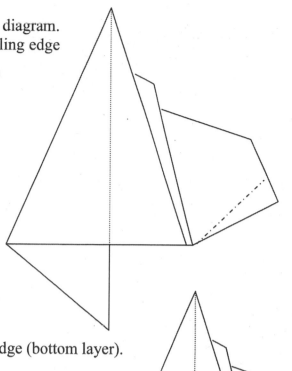

17. Valley fold and tuck trailing edge (bottom layer).

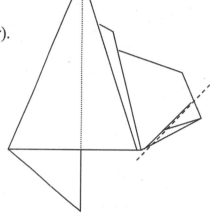

18. Valley fold top layer to the right.

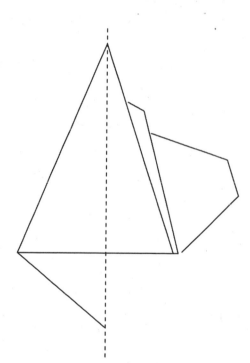

19. Valley fold and turn model sideways.

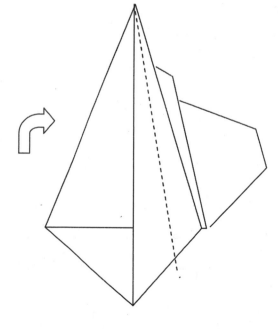

20. Model should look like this diagram.

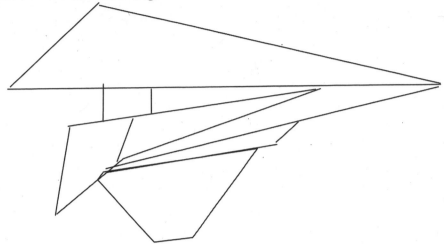

21. Fold the tiny valley fold (gray area) at the top first. Fold hard along the long valley fold.

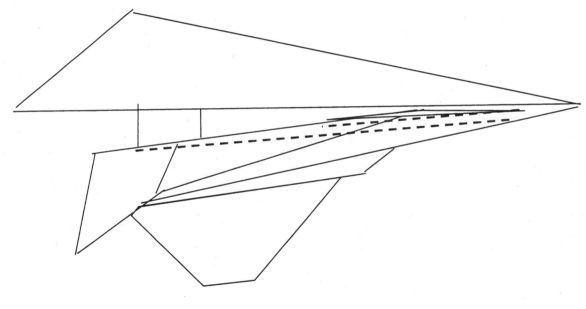

22. Fold up vertical fin/rudder.

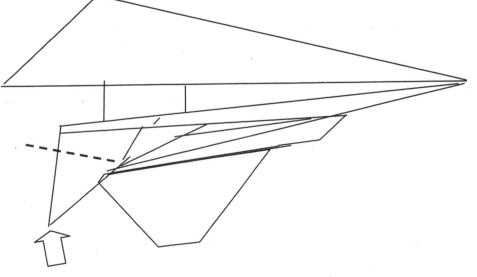

23. Mountain fold top layer while pivoting around point **A**. This produces a valley fold on the bottom layer.

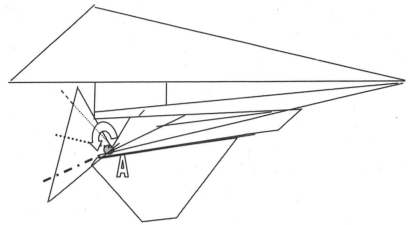

24. Fold down vertical fin/rudder.

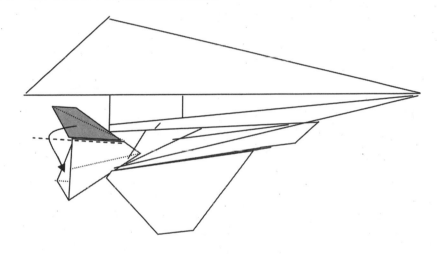

25. Repeat steps 10-24 for the left side.

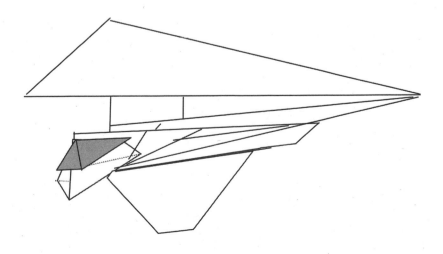

26. Reverse fold entire body through all layers.

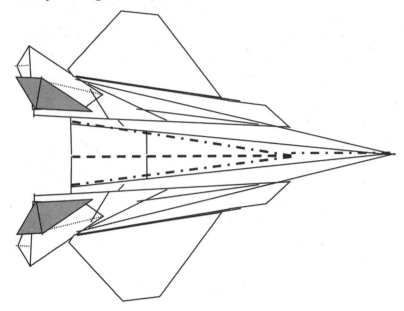

27. Mountain fold through all layers as indicated.

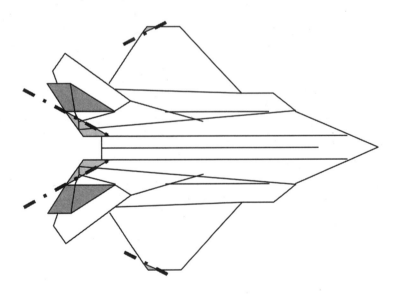

28. Details for finished aircraft architecture.

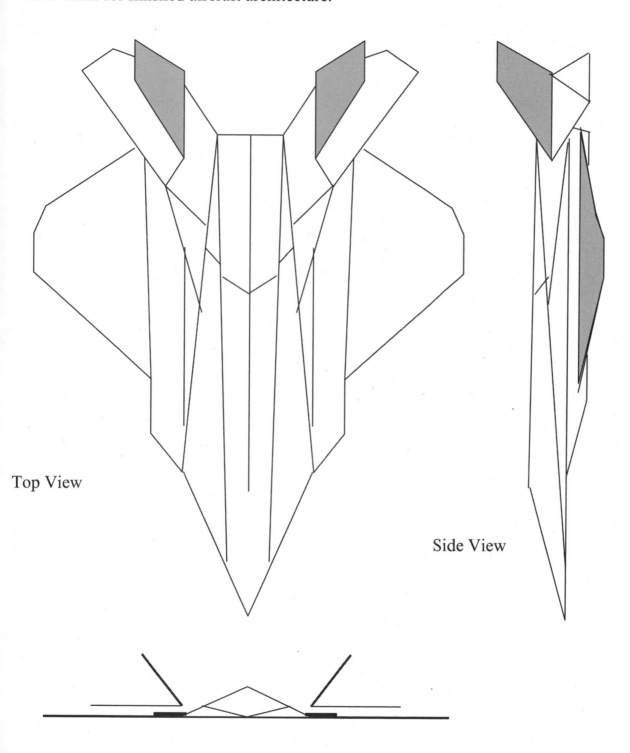

Top View

Side View

Front View

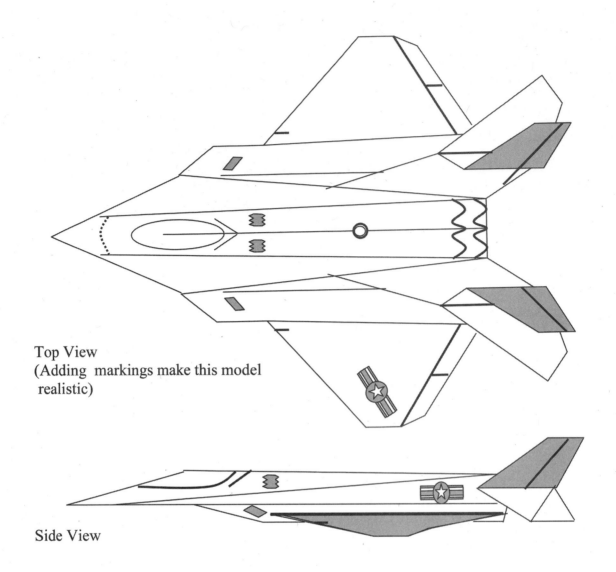

Top View
(Adding markings make this model
 realistic)

Side View

J-2 Experimental

The J-2 was Japan's version of the Me-163 German point interceptor. The J-2 was much larger and had two rocket engines (German made) instead of one, like the Me-163. It was to be used to defend the main island from a B-29 invasion, however, Japan surrendered while the first 25 J-2s were being assembled inside of a cavern carved in Mount Fuji.

Start with 8.5" x 11" rectangle colored side down

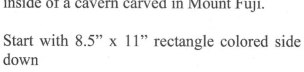

1. Valley fold along dashed lines, then unfold. (3 folds total)

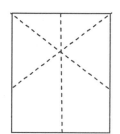

2. Mountain Fold along dash-dot line, then unfold and push sides to produce the following diagram.

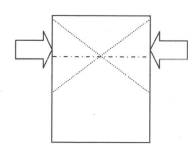

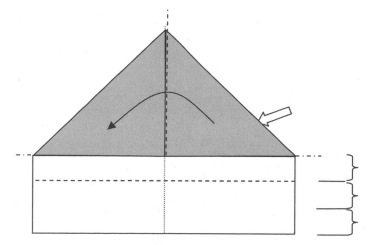

3. Valley fold and mountain fold where indicated (accordion fold). Lift top triangle layer and fold to the left.

4. Valley fold the diagonal bisector.

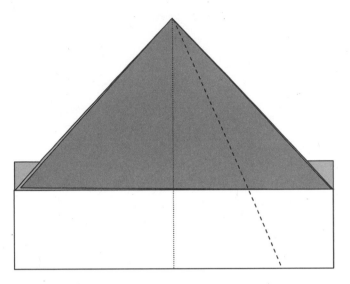

5. Twist fold around pivot point A. Lift top left triangle and move to the right.

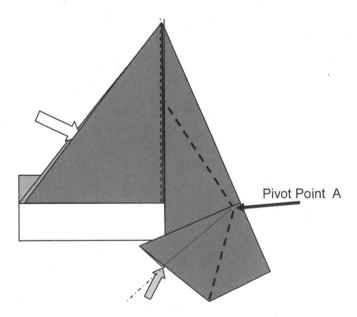

Pivot Point A

6. Valley fold top left triangle on bisector.

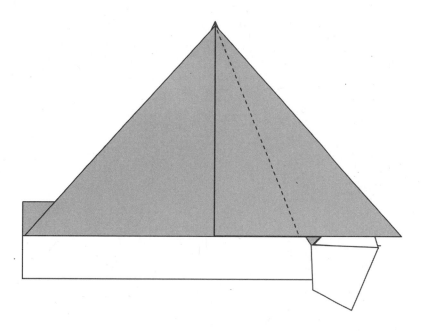

7. Fold top two layers over to the right and repeat steps 4 and 5 on the other side.

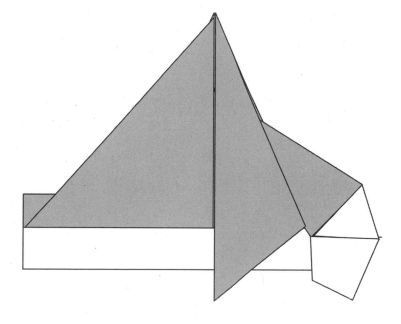

8. The result should look like this. Lift the top right layer and fold over to the left.

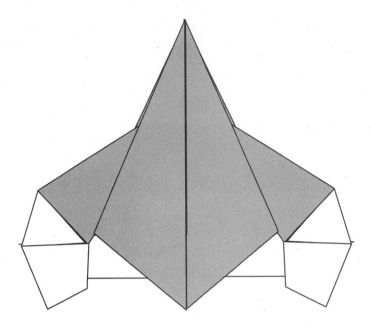

9. Off-set rabbit-ear fold the winglets along the dashed line on left and right side. (Just the top layer)

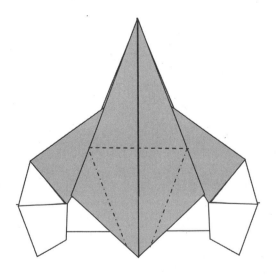

10. Mountain fold top layer each side to create winglets.

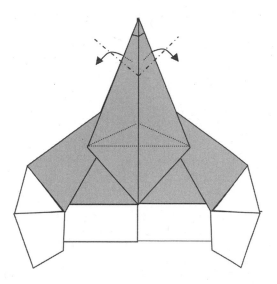

11. Pivot fold the bottom of the wings on each side.

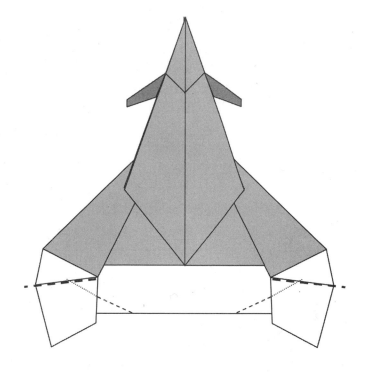

12. Valley-fold along the wing line on each side. This section may be carefully tucked under the top layer to make a clean wing. Valley fold rudder section.

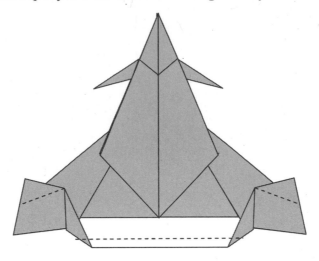

13. Turn the model over. Reverse fold the body to form the rudder.

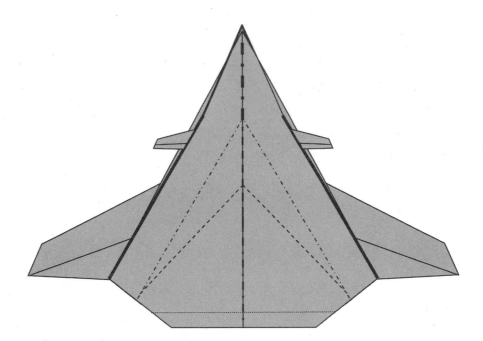

14. Valley fold the sides of body to make the wings level. Pull out the paper trapped in side vertical fin, then reverse fold.

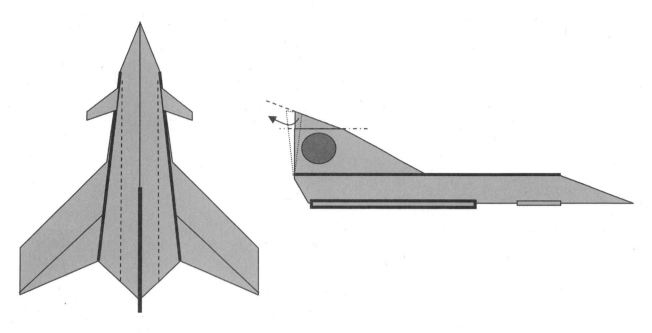

15. Finish according to the following drawings.

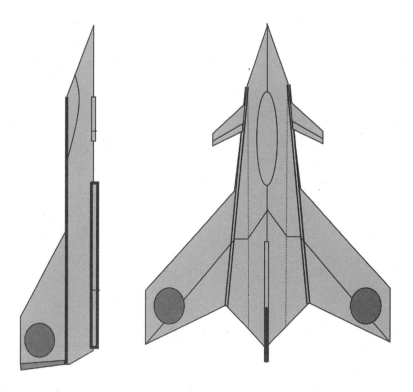

F-117 NIGHTHAWK

The mis-designated F-117, "F" indicates a "fighter," was actually a relatively slow bomber. It could only carry two Precision Guided Munitions (PGM) bombs and had no guns to protect itself. Its power laid in its invisibility to radar. The "F" designation assisted in recruiting the best fighter pilots to fly this seemingly vulnerable machine.

1. Start with 8.5" x 11" rectangle paper. Valley fold fold in half as shown.

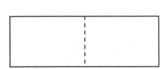

2. Valley fold in half again.

3. Valley fold in half on the diagonal (45 degrees) through one layer. Repeat on backside.

4. Lift the top layer.

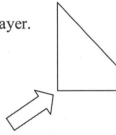

5. Lift center section and squash fold.

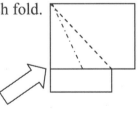

6. Should look like this. Unfold.

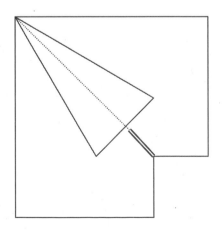

7. Refold so the top layer and bottom layer are symmetric. This will require all the bottom mountain and valley pre-folds to be reversed (i.e. if it is a mountain it will now be folded as a valley.) The top layer gets folded back into its original shape.

Petal fold top and bottom as indicated.

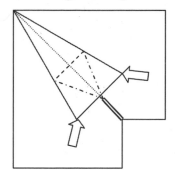

8. Stretch out Point(s) B and tuck Point A all the way inside. Repeat process on the bottom.

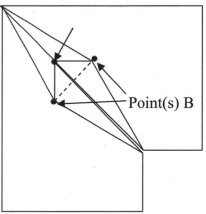

Point(s) B

9. Reverse fold wing tips. Use dotted line as guide.

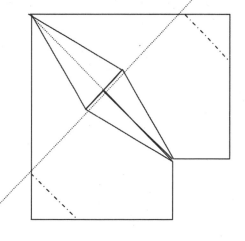

10. Mountain fold under top layer from point to point (creates elevons).

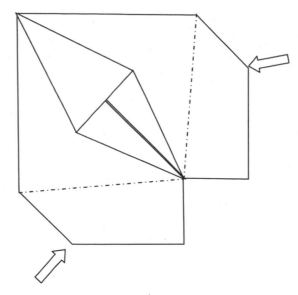

11. Mountain fold wings under as far as they will go. The edges will be square with the rest of the paper.

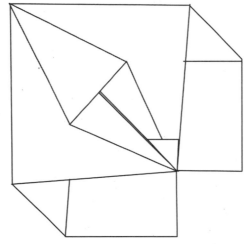

12. Turn model over. Mountain fold wings under (just top layer).

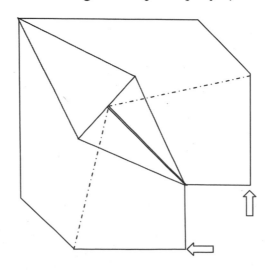

13. Fold model in half.
And turn 1/4.

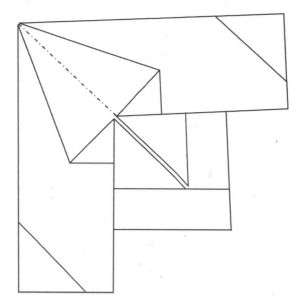

14. Mountain fold elevons and wings. Repeat on back side.

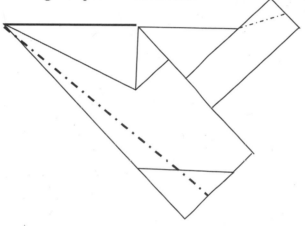

15. Tuck in rudders between top layer. Valley fold fuselage through all layers.
Valley fold elevons. Repeat on back side.

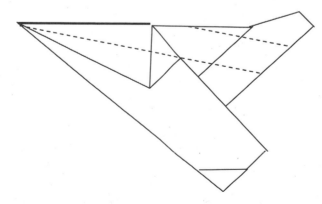

16. Mountain fold facets in fuselage. Mountain fold wings under. (top view)

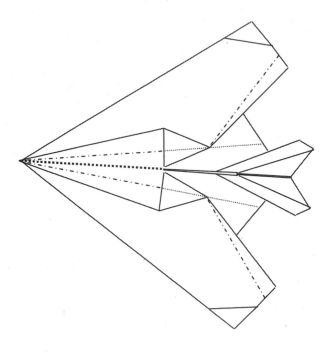

17. Make small reverse folds on wing tips.

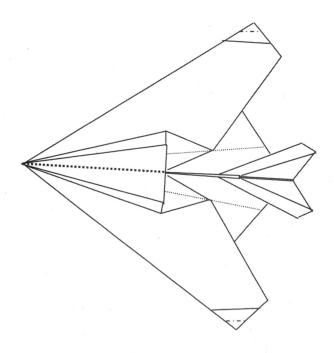

18. Trim up all folds for three dimensional effects.

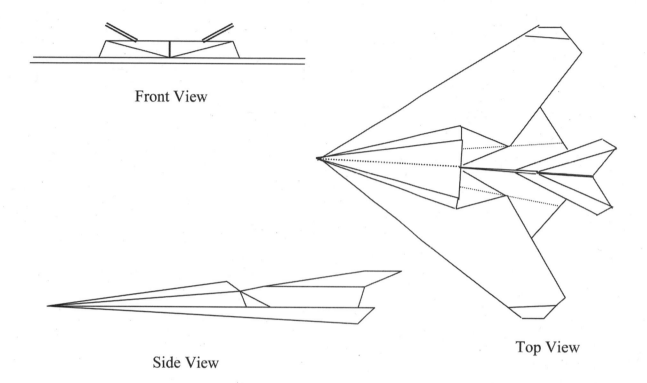

Front View

Side View

Top View

SR-71 Blackbird

The legendary SR-71 Blackbird set records for speed and altitude even as it was being decommissioned. It survived many years of service as a high-altitude reconnaissance vehicle and still inspires awe in its streamline features.

Start with 8.5" x 11" rectangle colored side down

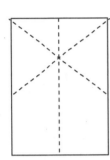

1. Valley fold along dashed lines, then unfold. (3 folds total) I leave 2 or three millimeters of paper on the leading edge. You may want to just fold to the corner diagonals.

2. Mountain fold along dash-dot line, then unfold and push sides to produce the following diagram. Push up on pre-fold at the bottom and leave folded.

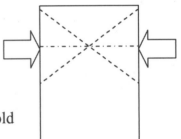

3. Valley fold the top layer (left and right).

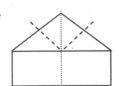

Expanded View

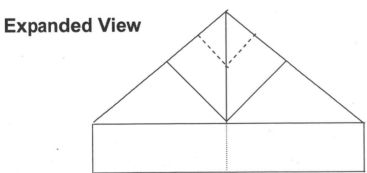

4. Valley fold left down along the edge.

5. Valley fold the piece shown and unfold.

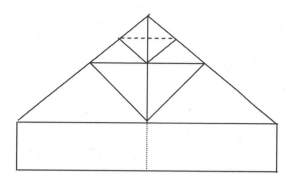

6. Unfold top layer.

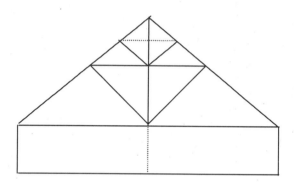

7. Valley fold left side, unfold. Repeat on the right side.

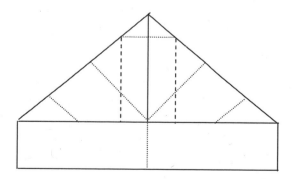

8. Use the folds from the previous steps to open the very top layer and extend the fuselage.

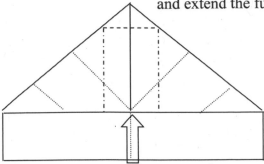

9. The result should look like this. Next fold both right and left sides as shown.

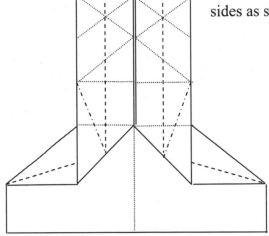

10. Turn the model over.

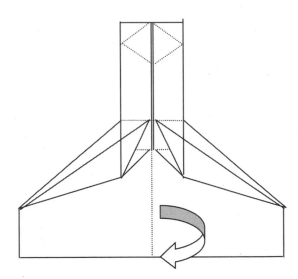

11. Fold and unfold the little triangle in half. This will be used as a marker for step 13.

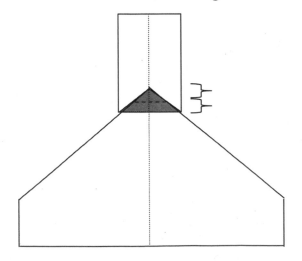

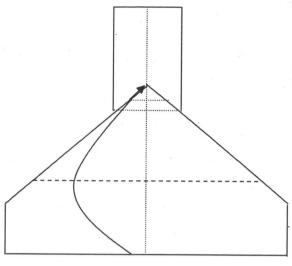

12. Fold a half of the top layer at the marker.

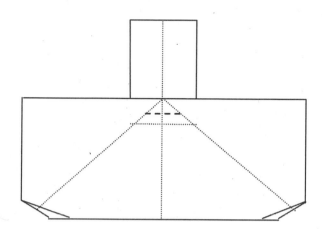

13. Valley fold to the tip of the little triangle.

14. Valley fold back to line back end to the mark.

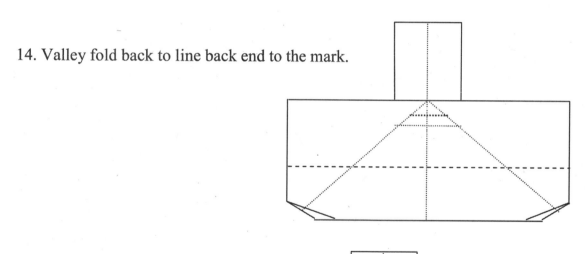

15. Reverse fold as indicated.

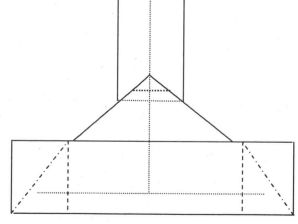

16. Fold the leading edge and unfold. The distance is the same as half the shaded triangle.

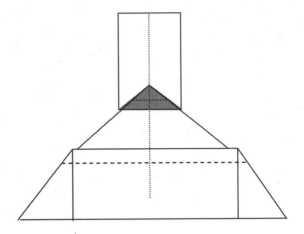

17. Unfold and sink along pre-folds from wingtip to wingtip.

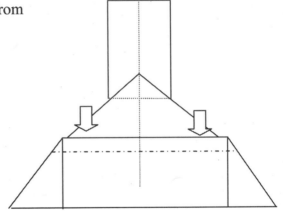

18. Valley fold rudders as indicated and tuck under top layer. Sink fold the gray triangle.

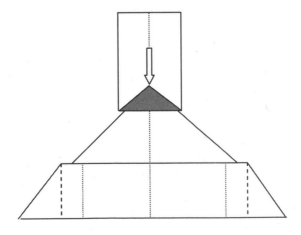

19. First pull out the trapped paper from inside of the wing. Then valley fold midway of nacelles.

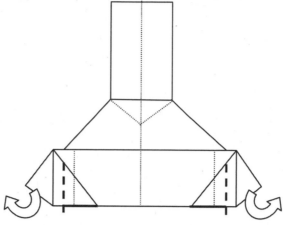

20. Unfold and refold as a reverse fold.

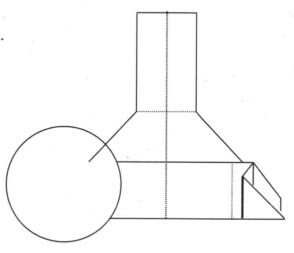

21. Here is the step 20 enlarged. Repeat on opposite side.

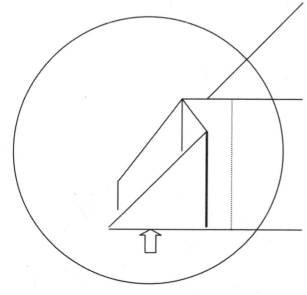

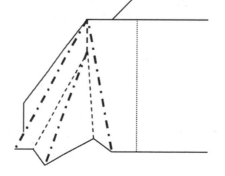

Open the triangle (rudder) and refold along the pre-fold lines as shown.

22. Mountain fold through all layers (both right and left side). Turn model over.

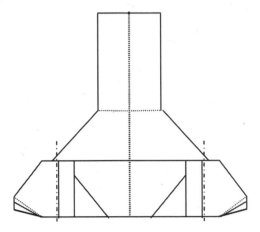

23. Valley fold nose (top layer). Valley fold winglets.

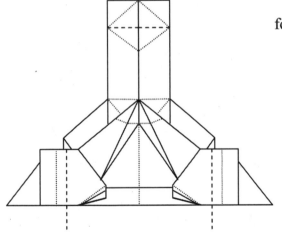

24. Petal fold the nose on both right and left sides.

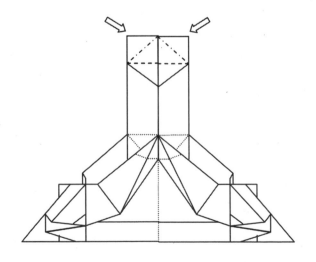

25. Valley fold the fuselage
at two-thirds from the center. Mountain
fold the wings outward.

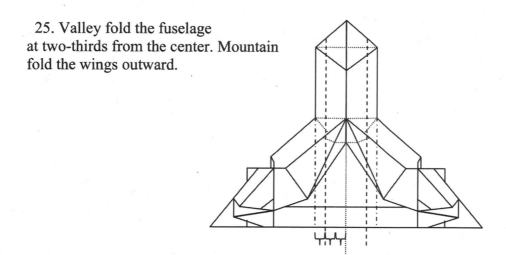

26. Valley fold in half
and give model a half turn.

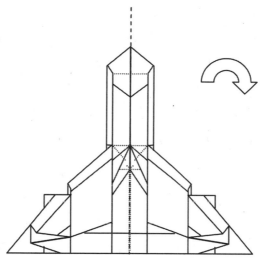

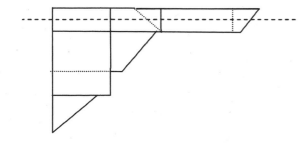

27. Valley fold fuselage on both sides
(many layers).

28. Reverse fold the nose section

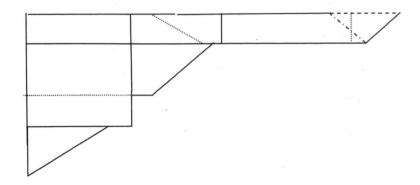

29. Small reverse fold.

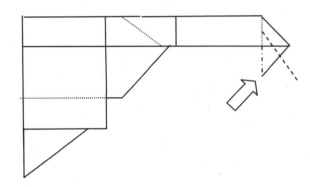

30. Valley fold fuselage in half at 90 degree angle, repeat behind.

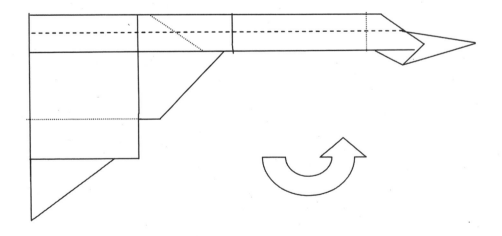

31. Fold the tips of the rudders with reverse fold.

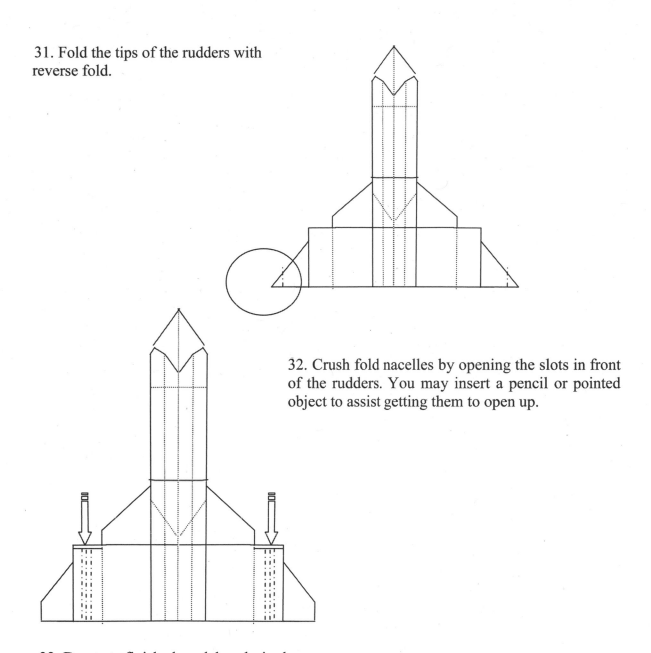

32. Crush fold nacelles by opening the slots in front of the rudders. You may insert a pencil or pointed object to assist getting them to open up.

33. Decorate finished model as desired.

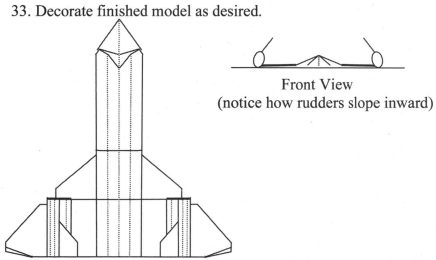

Front View
(notice how rudders slope inward)

WWII Aircraft Base

JU-87 Stuka/P-51 Mustang/Corsair/Spitfire/Zero

Start with square paper colored side up. Use at least a 10 inch square for the first attempt. Foil side up if using foil paper to produce a shiny model. Note: Foil model will retain the shape better and starting with the foil side down, ink markings may be added for additional realism.

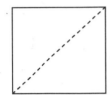

1. Valley fold along long diagonal.

2. Fold tip to tip just enough to mark the center.

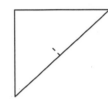

3. Fold top tip to center mark to mark the 1/4 length.

3a. For Stuka, make additional marks at 1/8 and 3/16ths as shown. Use the 3/16ths mark for creating base.

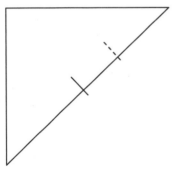

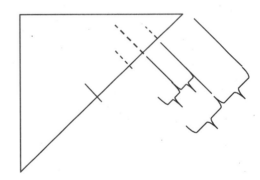

4. Unfold leaving colored side facing up.

5. Fold edge to 1/4 (3/16 for Stuka) mark and unfold. Repeat on top edge as shown. Unfold both edges.

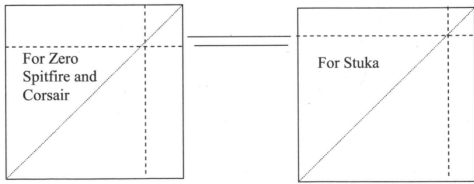

For Zero Spitfire and Corsair

For Stuka

6. Now re-fold both edges at the same time and pull resulting point on the upper right corner down to the right to look like this diagram.

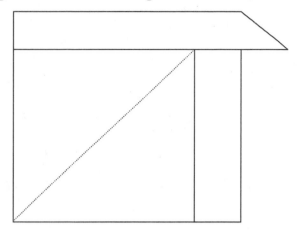

7. Squash fold corner.

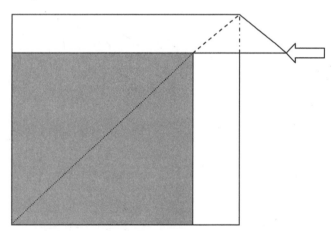

8. Valley fold flap. This will end up as the vertical fin and rudder.

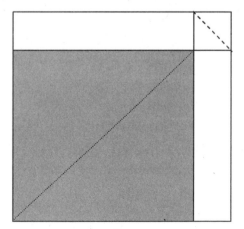

9. Fold edges outward along the valley fold line and raise the elevators to tuck excess under the elevator flaps.

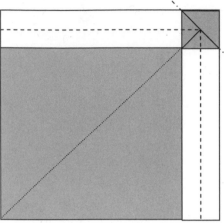

10. Mountain fold along centers as shown.
(Experts may now fold a bird-base and skip to Step 15)

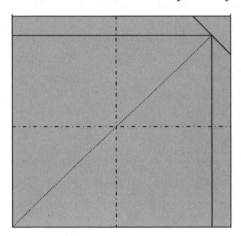

11. Valley fold along long diagonals and allow the assembly to collapse into a square. Keep rudder side up facing you.

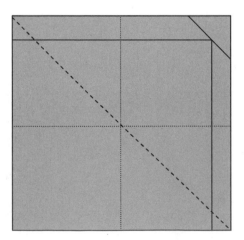

12. Perform valley pre-folds on both the front <u>and back</u> flaps. Fold point A to point B. Now unfold the folds that you just made. NOTE: There many layers on the front side, so fold tight and crisp.

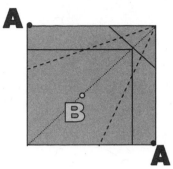

13. Petal fold front. The mountain folds were the valley folds of the prior . This is a tricky fold on the rudder side. Allow the paper to collapse naturally around the stabilator assembly and neaten up all edges to look like the diagram in 13.

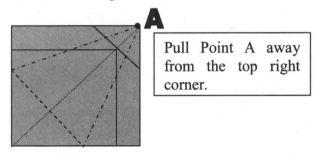

Pull Point A away from the top right corner.

14. Valley fold the tips back together.

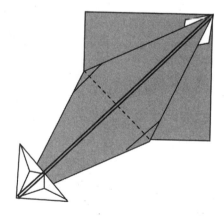

15. Model should look like this. Turn the model over.

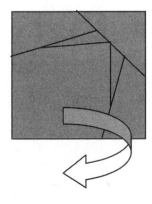

16. Petal fold the back side. This should be much easier.

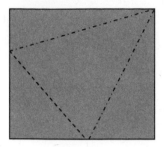

17. Valley fold tip back up.

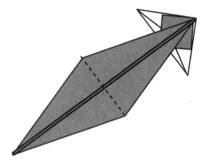

18. Turn model (135 degrees) from this position to position in diagram in 18.

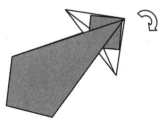

19. Valley fold tip on front and back.

20. Valley fold down at one third from the base of hidden triangle, front and back.

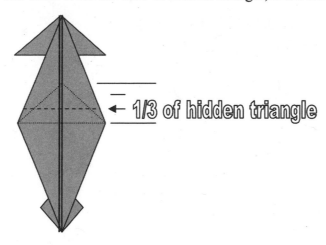

21. Fold left rear flap around to the right and fold right top flap over to the left.

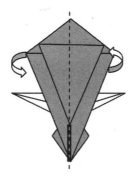

22. Fold wing tips up. Front and back.

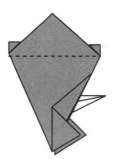

23. Fold wings down at 1/3 of hidden triangle. Front and back.

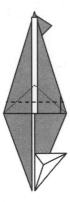

24. Raise both the front end and the back end with pinch folds. Pull out on the front end and make it line up with the bottom of model. Do the same for the back end except raise it to line up with the 1/3 mark as shown in diagram on 25.

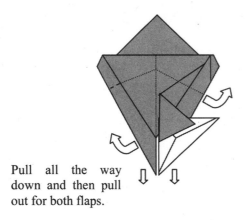

Pull all the way down and then pull out for both flaps.

25. Reverse fold the front end and valley fold the rear of fuselage both front and back.

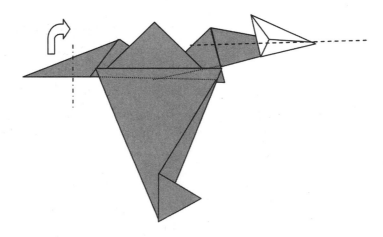

26. Reverse fold the leading edge of wing. Pull out aileron flap. Valley fold nose section. Repeat all three of these folds on the backside.

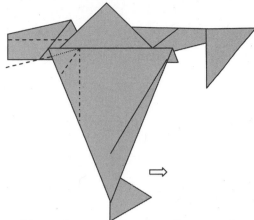

27. Mountain fold the trailing edge to make the aileron and tuck the corner into the bottom layer under the wing. Repeat behind.

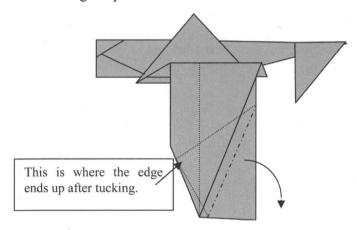

This is where the edge ends up after tucking.

28. Do a similar fold as with the front of the wings. Repeat behind. Pull out the hidden triangle in the front and reverse fold to make nose cone.

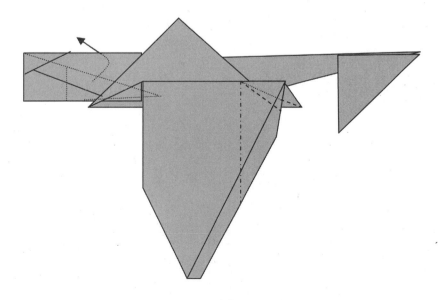

29. Valley fold the wings up and allow the valley folds to form on the leading and trailing edges. (Front and back) To improve the finish, ensure that they line up evenly.

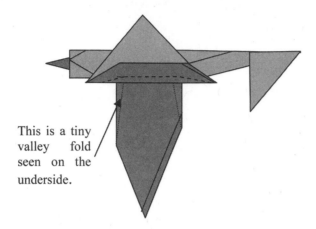

This is a tiny valley fold seen on the underside.

30. Valley fold the tiny triangles until the wings are horizontal. (Front and Back)

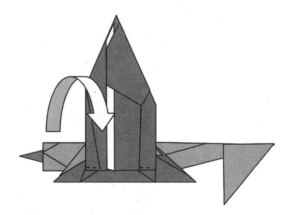

31. Thick black line indicates profile view of wing. Preliminary fold cockpit by valley fold as indicated.

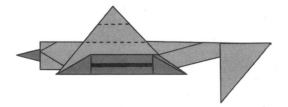

32. Spread squash fold the small square made by the top line. Note: The top line will be mountain folded while the bottom line in the above will be valley folded (on both sides). Now mountain fold the center of the square while pulling up and carefully form the cockpit.

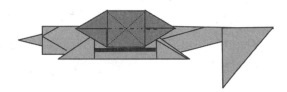

33. Pinch fold rudder by pulling only one layer of paper up at point A and letting it roll along the fuselage.

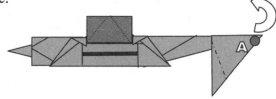

34. Form the rudder and elevator reverse folds. Make the tail wheel by folding under the remaining white triangle.

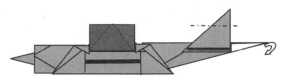

35. This is the WWII Fighter Aircraft Base. From this point on the model may be shaped into a German Ju-87 Stuka, P-51 Mustang, US Navy Corsair, British Supermarine Spitfire, Japanese Zero, or other propeller drive aircraft of similar design.

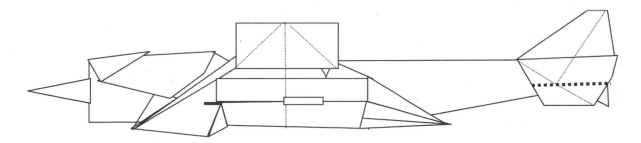

German Ju-87 Stuka: Fold the wings as indicated. Try to make the folds symmetrical as possible by pinching the wing tips as these folds are made. Wrap the paper gently around the shaded area on the tail. (Partly unfold to keep from tearing the paper)

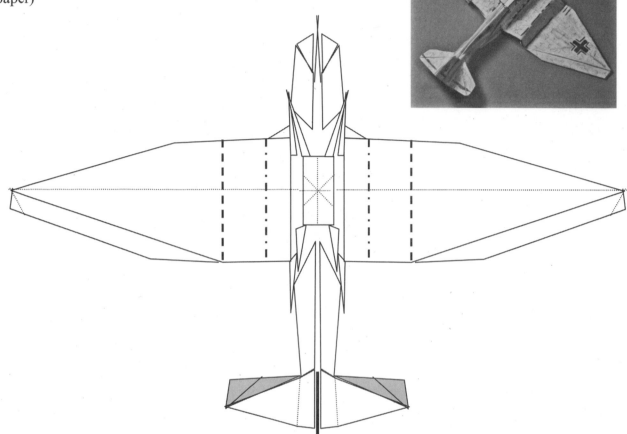

Finish model as shown and decorate to suit taste.

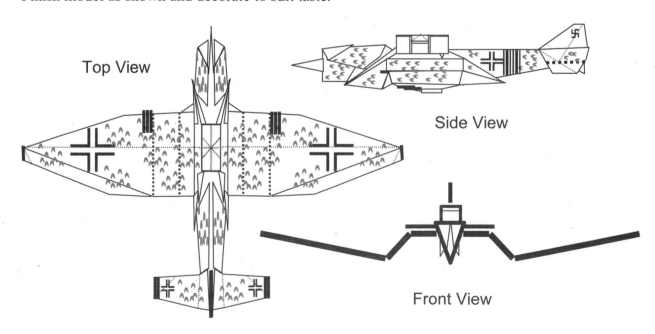

Top View

Side View

Front View

US Navy Corsair: round wing tips out. Fold the wings as indicated, but not crisply, use soft folds. Try to make the folds symmetrical as possible by pinching the wing tips as these folds are made. Wrap around the shaded area on the tail. Shape canopy rounded and smaller than Stuka.

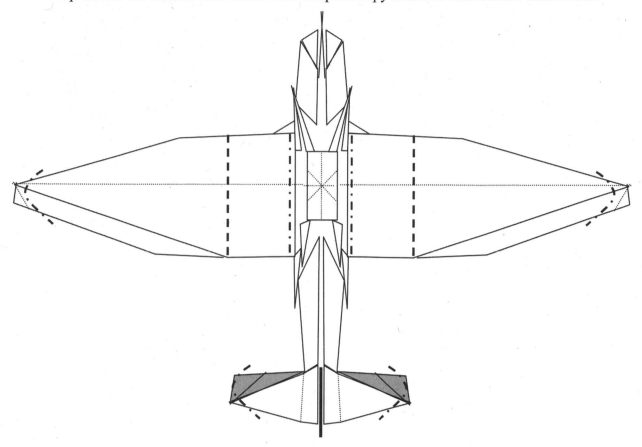

Finish model as shown and decorate to suit taste.

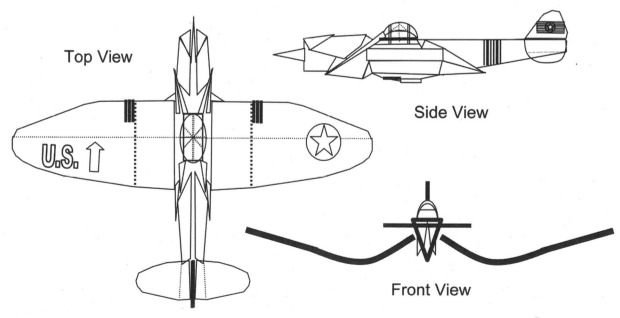

Top View

Side View

Front View

British Supermarine Spitfire: Wrap paper at tail (gray area) so that it is all one surface. Round wing and wing tips by making many tiny mountain folds.

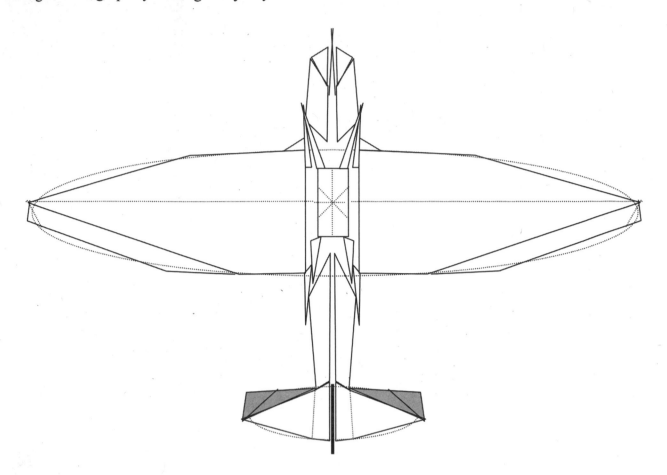

Finish model as shown and decorate to suit taste. Note the aesthetic elliptical wing. This will require numerous small mountain-folds to produce a nice result.

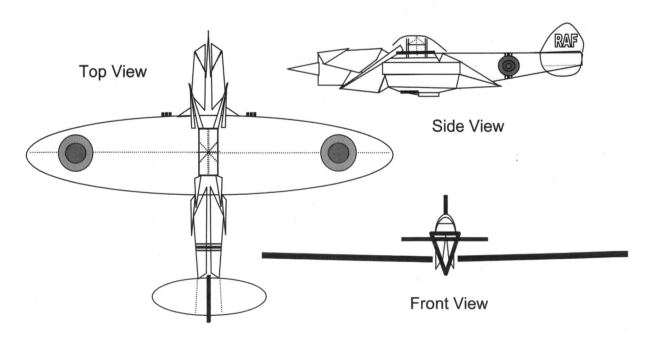

Top View

Side View

Front View

Japanese Zero: round wing and wing tips.

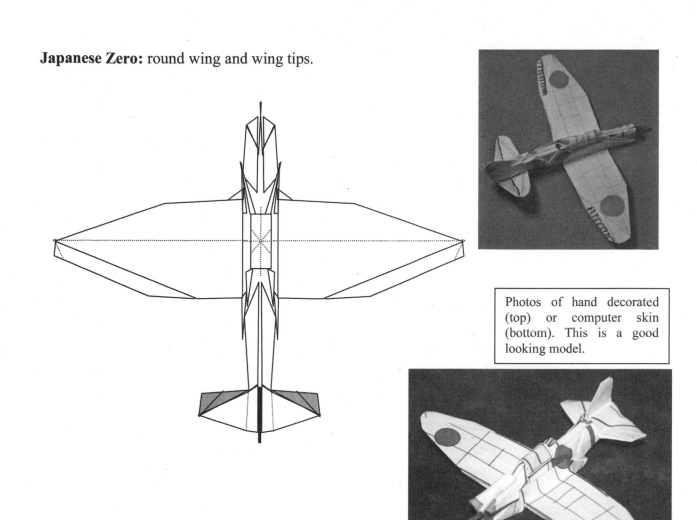

Photos of hand decorated (top) or computer skin (bottom). This is a good looking model.

Finish model as shown and decorate to suit taste.

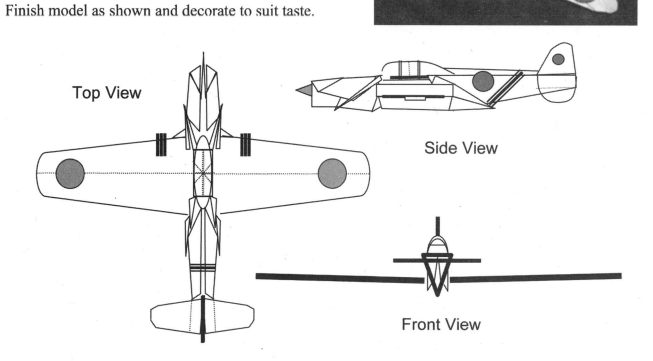

Top View

Side View

Front View

A-10 Warthog

The A-10 Warthog was originally designed as a tank killer. Nearing its useful life, the first Gulf War used the A-10 with Precision Guided Munitions (PGM) and ensured its long term viability as a staple for the national defense.

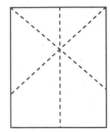

1. Start with 8.5" x 11" rectangle paper. Color side down fold and unfold as shown.

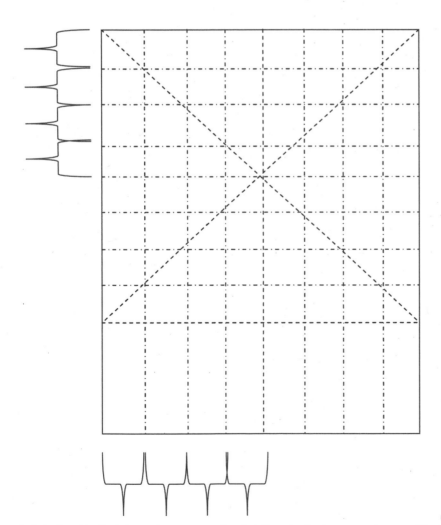

2. Mark 1/8 divisions by mountain-folding in halves as shown. Unfold completely.

3. Mark the 1/16 portions of the tail and the 3/16 margins from each edge of the square as shown.

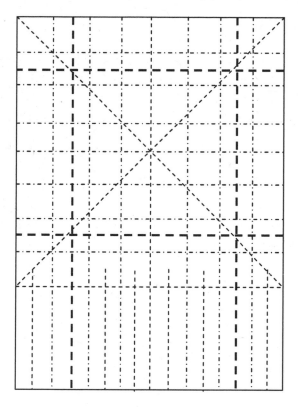

4. Double-sink fold as shown. Note that this is a tricky fold and requires some patience. Be sure that the results look like the diagram in number 5.

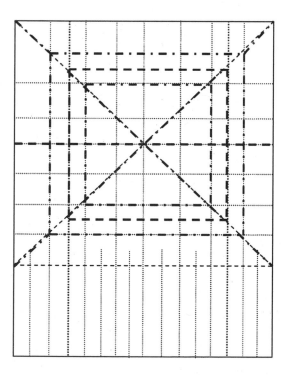

5. Fold like an accordion as shown. Note that there is a layer below that will soon be the wings.

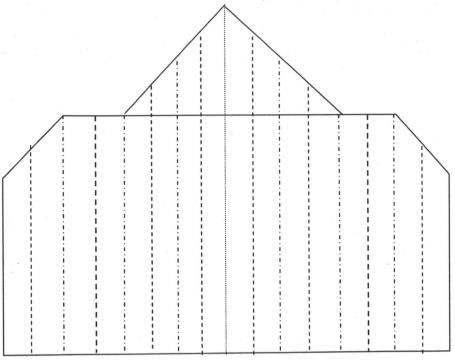

6. Fold bottom layer on left and right side. Tuck under top layer.

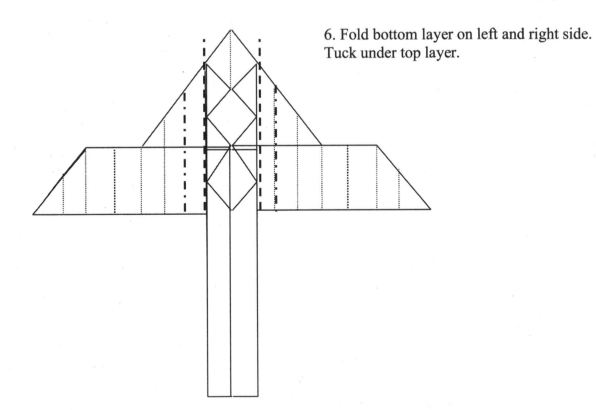

7. Fold point A down to point B. the paper will invert along the pre-folds.

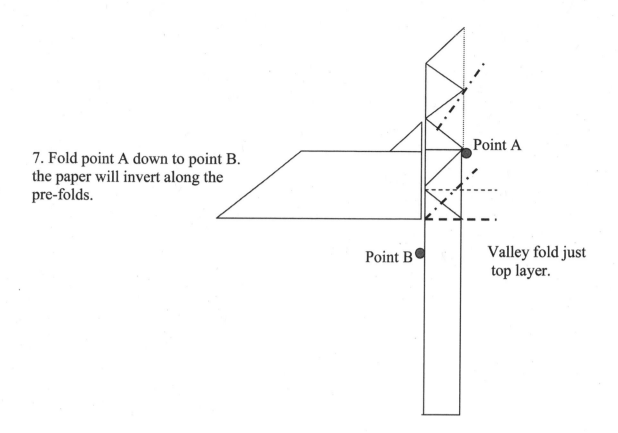

Point A

Point B

Valley fold just top layer.

Repeat on the right side. Result should look like 8.

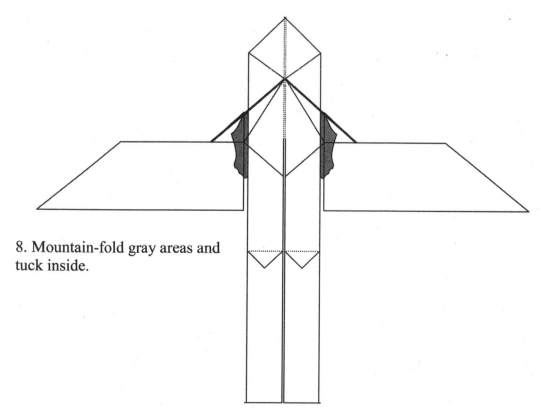

8. Mountain-fold gray areas and tuck inside.

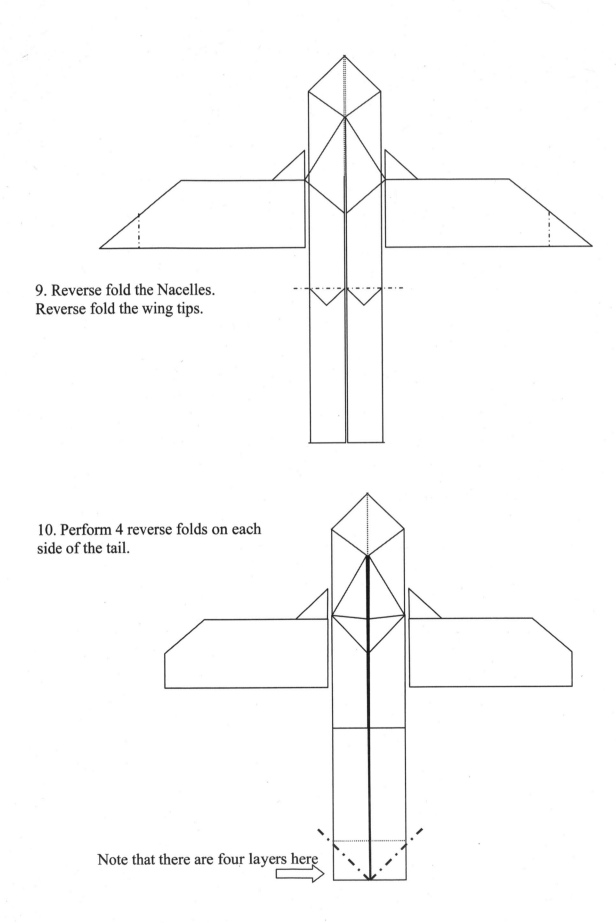

9. Reverse fold the Nacelles.
Reverse fold the wing tips.

10. Perform 4 reverse folds on each
side of the tail.

Note that there are four layers here

11. Fold point A to point B by stretching top 3 layers and hanging onto the last layer's point. The 4th layer's point will invert and disappear. Repeat on left side.

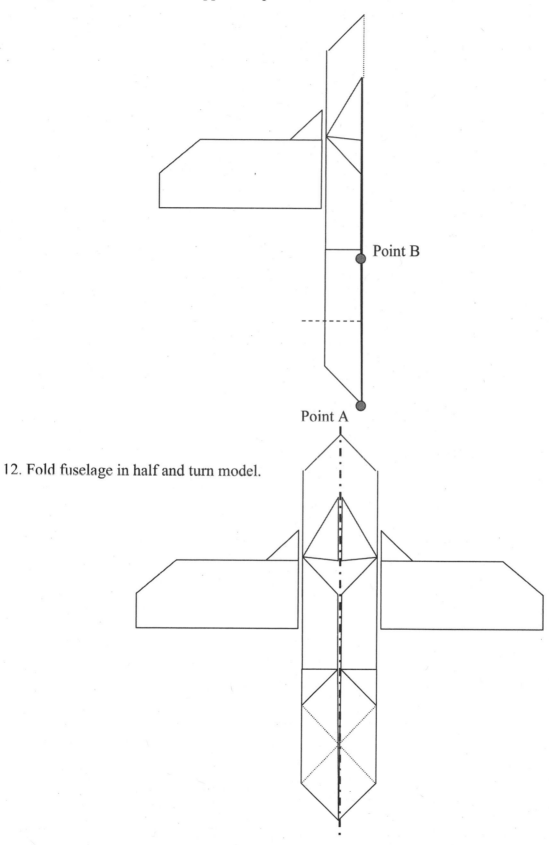

Point B

Point A

12. Fold fuselage in half and turn model.

13. Reverse fold entire tail section. Fold down top layer of nose section. Repeat on back side.

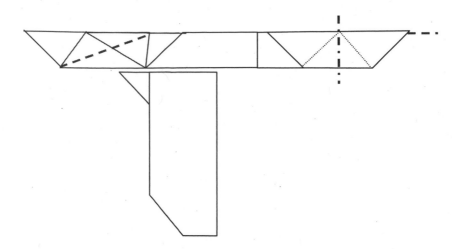

14. Fold Point A to Point B on elevator to vertical on front and back. Mountain fold the nose on both sides.

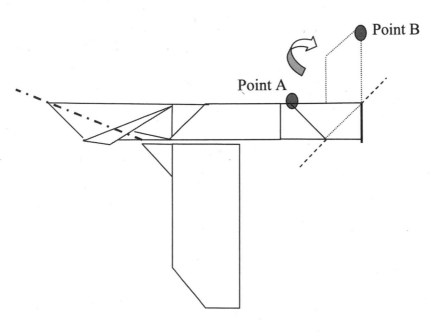

15. Fold down elevators, front and back.

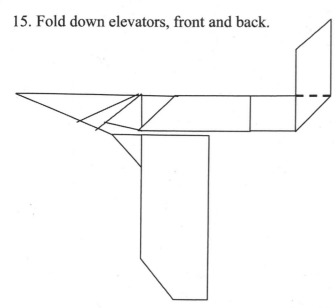

16. Fold up tip, front and back.

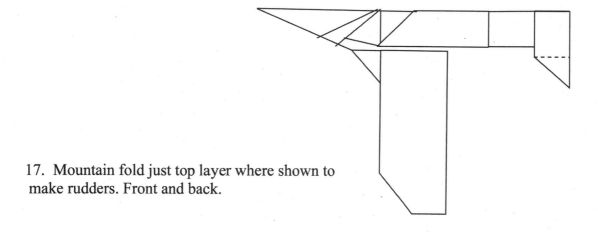

17. Mountain fold just top layer where shown to make rudders. Front and back.

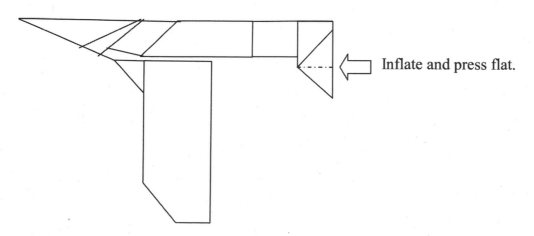

Inflate and press flat.

18. Raise wings
to 90 degrees and do
a half reverse fold
on the nose.

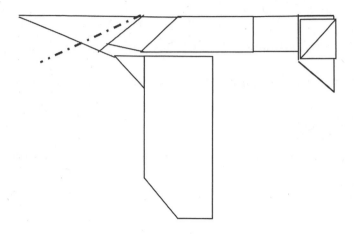

19. Fold up elevator and finish as shown in 3-D views.

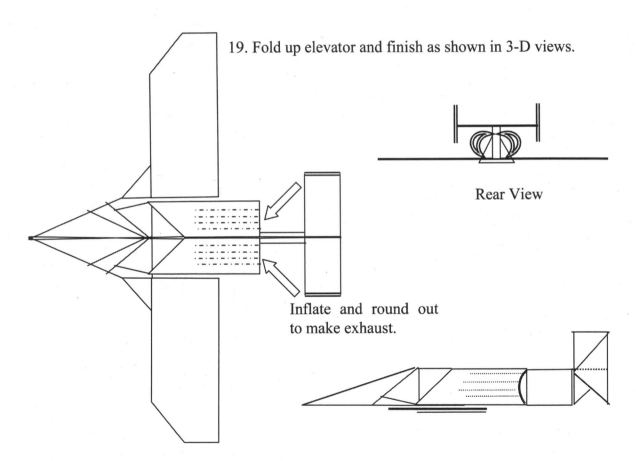

Rear View

Inflate and round out
to make exhaust.

How to Trim/Airplane Terms

Trimming paper airplanes is much like trimming full-scale aircraft. Small adjustments to the edge of the wings and stabilator (combination of rudder and elevator) make big changes to the flight path. A properly trimmed airplane will fly longer and straighter. I recommend you keep the wings or canards and the rudders straight and neat as possible and only adjust the elevators as shown to control the flight path.

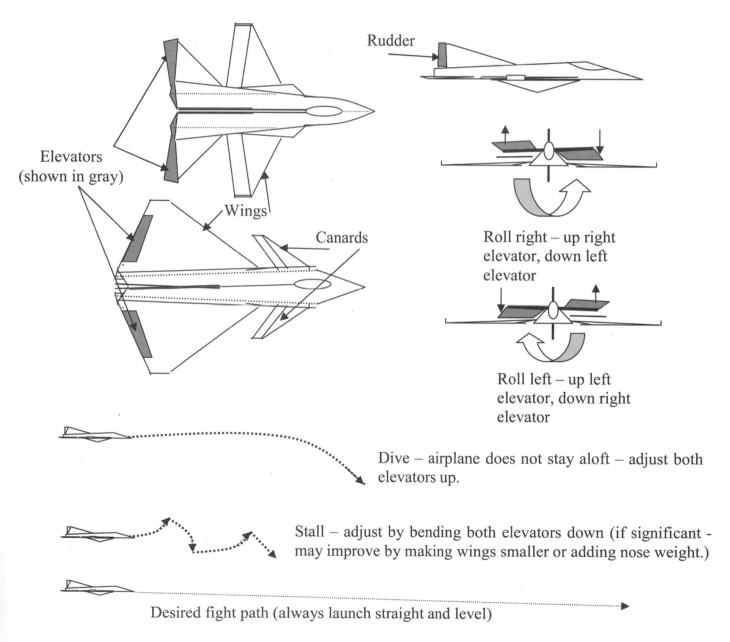

Rudder

Elevators
(shown in gray)

Wings

Canards

Roll right – up right elevator, down left elevator

Roll left – up left elevator, down right elevator

Dive – airplane does not stay aloft – adjust both elevators up.

Stall – adjust by bending both elevators down (if significant - may improve by making wings smaller or adding nose weight.)

Desired fight path (always launch straight and level)

Further Study/Bibliography

Tem Boun, *Awesome Origami Aircraft Models of the World's Best Fighters*, Victoria, BC, Trafford Publishing, 2005.
 Excellent aircraft (non-flying). Should be made of foil or foil back paper. Unusual paper dimensions (3:1, 3.5:1) long and thin.

Peter Engel, *Folding the Universe: Origami from Angelfish to Zen*, New York, Vintage Books, 1989.
 Unusual study into creativity, chaos theory, and patterns. Although there are no aircraft, the animals are great. Complex designs and square sheets only.

Robert J. Lang, *Origami Design Secrets*, Natick, MA, A K Peters, Ltd., 2003.
 Remarkable in-depth mathematical study on creating origami designs. Squares only, no aircraft.

John Montroll, *Origami for the Enthusiast*, New York, Dover Publications, 1988.
 Outstanding folder and design technique, however, only animals no aircraft. Squares only.

Thay Yang, *Exotic Paper Airplanes* (1998) and *Exquisite Interceptors* (2000), Fort Bragg, CA, Cypress House.
 Excellent books on concept aircraft. All designs are 8.5 inches by 11 inches.

For addition information on the aircraft and their history:

David Donald, *The Complete Encyclopedia of World Aircraft*, New York, Barnes and Noble, Orbis Publishing Ltd., 1997.

Jay Miller, *The X-Planes: X-1 to X-45*, Midland Publishing, Hinckley, England, 2001.

Jim Winchester, *X-Planes and Prototypes*, New York, Barnes and Noble, Amber Books, Ltd, 2005.